# GOLF ANATOMY

## Craig Davies
## Vince DiSaia, CSCS

**Human Kinetics**

**Library of Congress Cataloging-in-Publication Data**

Davies, Craig.
 Golf anatomy / Craig Davies, Vince DiSaia.
  p. cm.
 ISBN-13: 978-0-7360-8434-5 (soft cover)
 ISBN-10: 0-7360-8434-7 (soft cover)
 1. Golf--Training. 2. Golf--Physiological aspects. 3. Biomechanics. I. DiSaia, Vince. II. Title.
 GV979.T68.D38 2010
 796.352--dc22

                                      2009054271

ISBN-10: 0-7360-8434-7 (print)
ISBN-13: 978-0-7360-8434-5 (print)

This publication is written and published to provide accurate and authoritative information relevant to the subject matter presented. It is published and sold with the understanding that the author and publisher are not engaged in rendering legal, medical, or other professional services by reason of their authorship or publication of this work. If medical or other expert assistance is required, the services of a competent professional person should be sought.

**Acquisitions Editor:** Tom Heine; **Developmental Editors:** Amanda Eastin-Allen, Cynthia McEntire; **Assistant Editor:** Laura Podeschi; **Copyeditor:** Patricia MacDonald; **Graphic Designer:** Fred Starbird; **Graphic Artist:** Francine Hamerski; **Cover Designer:** Keith Blomberg; **Photographer (for illustration references):** Neil Bernstein; **Visual Production Assistant:** Joyce Brumfield; **Art Manager:** Kelly Hendren; **Associate Art Manager:** Alan L. Wilborn; **Illustrator (cover):** Jennifer Gibas; **Illustrators (interior):** Dragonfly Media Group, Precision Graphics, and Jennifer Gibas; **Printer:** United Graphics

Human Kinetics books are available at special discounts for bulk purchase. Special editions or book excerpts can also be created to specification. For details, contact the Special Sales Manager at Human Kinetics.

Printed in the United States of America   10 9 8 7 6 5 4 3

The paper in this book is certified under a sustainable forestry program.

**Human Kinetics**
Web site: www.HumanKinetics.com

*United States:* Human Kinetics
P.O. Box 5076
Champaign, IL 61825-5076
800-747-4457
e-mail: humank@hkusa.com

*Canada:* Human Kinetics
475 Devonshire Road Unit 100
Windsor, ON N8Y 2L5
800-465-7301 (in Canada only)
e-mail: info@hkcanada.com

*Europe:* Human Kinetics
107 Bradford Road
Stanningley
Leeds LS28 6AT, United Kingdom
+44 (0) 113 255 5665
e-mail: hk@hkeurope.com

*Australia:* Human Kinetics
57A Price Avenue
Lower Mitcham, South Australia 5062
08 8372 0999
e-mail: info@hkaustralia.com

*New Zealand:* Human Kinetics
P.O. Box 80
Torrens Park, South Australia 5062
0800 222 062
e-mail: info@hknewzealand.com

E4825

# CONTENTS

# FOREWORD

Playing against the world's best golfers on the PGA Tour requires extreme mental and physical conditioning. During the 2009 season, my conditioning allowed me to make the cut in 24 out of 25 tournaments, finish 16th on the PGA Tour's money list, and represent my country on the victorious U.S. President's Cup team. To achieve these results and this level of consistency requires that every aspect of my golf game run on all cylinders.

The most notable change that has occurred in professional golf in the past decade is the necessity for players to maximize their physical skill sets. The fitness trailer that travels with the PGA Tour is busier every year as players attempt to maintain or gain an edge over their peers. Since starting to work with my good friend, Dr. Craig Davies, a few years ago, I have paid more attention to the fitness, nutrition, and physical side of my game. During tournament weeks, I make sure to warm up effectively for about 30 minutes prior to both my tournament rounds and pretournament practice sessions. I also make sure to spend the appropriate amount of time each day when I have finished play on my fitness regime and preventive physical therapy. My weekly program during the season is as much about increasing my performance as preventing injuries. As we all know, golf is a repetitive and stressful sport that can create a great deal of wear and tear on the body if you do not take care of yourself properly. Whether you are talking about professionals or weekend amateurs, it is not uncommon for at least one of the players in a foursome to use pain relievers to help him through a round. If you take care of your body, you should not have to rely on pain relievers.

While it is important to focus on golf fitness during the season, the off-season is when I have the chance to really make major changes to my physical skill sets. I think this is an important concept for both the amateur and professional player, especially those who live in colder climates and are not able to play golf during the winter. The off-season is the perfect time to really focus on your golf fitness and make changes to your body that will help develop your game in both the short and long term.

*Golf Anatomy* does a great job breaking down the various skill sets (balance, mobility, stability, strength, and power) and injury prevention exercises into simple-to-follow progressions. I have worked with Dr. Craig Davies for a number of years now, and many of the exercises you see within the pages of this book are the very same ones I have used in my own development. I encourage you to pay specific attention to the form you use during the application of these exercises and remind you not to rush through them. These exercises have made the difference in my game, and they can for you, too.

**Hunter Mahan**

# PREFACE

The drastic increase in the popularity of golf over the past couple decades has spawned a revolution in the production of high-tech golf equipment and training devices. Everyone is seeking that magical new club, ball, or training aid that will help him hit the ball farther and score lower. However, in the past 30 years, even with all the improvements in ball and equipment technology, there has been *no* change in the average North American handicap. One major reason for this is that golfers, unlike other athletes, spend minimal time and energy improving their bodies' ability to properly move within the golf swing. Without this key ingredient, a golfer will not only fall short of his potential but will also put himself at high risk of injury.

When attempting to improve their game, golfers spend endless time and money on clubs and lessons without first improving the most efficient tool available to them: *their own bodies*. All golfers are interested in increasing distance, accuracy, and consistency, but they always look to do that with an expensive new club or a new and improved ball. However, faster and more lasting gains in all three of these areas can be achieved by improving physical fitness to allow the body to perform the necessary movements for an effective, powerful golf swing. Once this fitness is achieved, swing lessons become more efficient, new clubs hit farther than ever, and golf ultimately becomes much more fun.

Fortunately, the importance of physical fitness for golf has begun to gain more attention. Tiger Woods' incredible workout regimes and consistency on the course have helped the fitness aspect of the game to begin earning the respect it deserves. However, even with this heightened awareness, most golfers are still ultimately unsure of what muscles are actually used in golf and how these muscles affect each and every swing. This unfortunately leaves golfers with an incomplete knowledge base and does not allow for workouts executed with specific purpose and in direct relation to the golf swing itself.

In *Golf Anatomy*, all of these connections are easily made so that you can have a clear and concise understanding of how your body functions during the golf swing. You will also learn how to train specific areas and understand how each one will directly assist in improving your golf game. Never before has a book so clearly and easily linked the two worlds of fitness and golf. Having the ability to fully understand each step of the process makes the learning and training experience more fulfilling, more motivational, more effective, and much more fun.

This book has ultimately been designed for a few different reasons. First and foremost, every golfer should have a basic understanding of how a proper golf swing functions. This is why the first chapter is dedicated to improving your knowledge of the basic key elements of a good golf swing. These are many of the same things that golf instructors look for in their students and strive to improve upon to produce a better golfer. The true complexity of the golf swing could never be covered in one chapter, but grasping the main points mentioned in chapter 1 of *Golf Anatomy* will help you appreciate how forces are created in the golf swing and why it is so important to have a body fit for golf. Illustrations let you see what proper swing technique looks like as well as give you an inside view of what the muscles are doing at each point in the swing.

The second main reason for this book is to provide you with a clear and detailed picture of the muscles being used both during the golf swing and within various exercises. After all, the more you know, the better you can prepare. Detailed anatomical illustrations are provided for both the fitness section and golf swing section to show you exactly what is going on within the body during each movement, both on and off the course. The anatomical illustrations that accompany the exercises are color coded to indicate the primary and secondary muscles and connective tissues featured in each exercise and movement.

This intimate look into the body allows you to quickly understand not only which muscles are being worked in each exercise but also how those same muscles are utilized directly in the golf swing itself. This straightforward illustrated connection is unique to *Golf Anatomy*, and it is the easiest way to learn about both the body and the golf swing and how they so closely influence one another.

Third, this book was written to present you with numerous concise exercises that will help improve the mobility, stability, balance, strength, and power of the muscles that directly affect the accuracy, distance, and consistency of your golf swing. These will be presented through step-by-step instructions so that you can easily perform each exercise. Having these instructions combined with detailed anatomical illustrations allows you to train with a purpose and be able to understand how that training translates directly to your swing. Your own body is the most powerful and effective piece of equipment you can use on the golf course. The more knowledge and understanding you have of this tool, the more effectively you can use and improve upon it.

Another major benefit this book provides is information on preventing injuries. The golf swing is one of the most dynamic, explosive, and complex movements in all of sport. The golfer's body produces and absorbs some of the highest forces seen in the athletic world. This is evident in the fact that up to 80 percent of all golfers will experience *at least* one injury during the course of their golfing careers. Considering that more than 35 million people play golf in the United States alone, that amounts to more than 28 million injuries. One reason for the high injury rate is that the forces created in the golf swing produce up to eight times a golfer's body weight in compressive forces to the spine. To put that into perspective, running—which is considered a high-impact activity that causes stress to the body—produces only three to four times a runner's body weight in compressive forces to the spine. The spine is just one of the many body parts that require both strength and mobility to endure the repeated high-velocity forces of each golf swing. Having to absorb all of these stresses with each swing is reason enough to keep your body as fit, strong, and active as possible. Inability to withstand such forces will lead to dangerous compensations, poor swing technique, and injury. Fitness helps prevent injury and promotes optimal performance on the golf course.

Although improving your physical fitness for better golf performance and reduced risk of injury is an important goal, it is not enough for us to just give you dozens of exercises and have you train at random. For this reason, the outline of *Golf Anatomy* was designed to help you understand the anatomy involved in the golf swing and how it can be used most effectively. Since you are training to improve fitness for a sport, not just to get bigger muscles, it only makes sense to arrange the chapters of *Golf Anatomy* in a *functionally* logical order. This unique approach to training was designed specifically with the golfer in mind and can be found only in this book.

Because of the dynamic nature of the golf swing, many parts of the body need to be stabilized while others are moving at high speeds. Golf definitely necessitates speed, strength, and power, but none of these can be effectively achieved without first having sufficient mobility, balance, and stability. These last three are the building blocks on which the first three depend. For this reason, the early chapters of this book focus on the mobility, stability, and balance of the golfer's body, and we have left strength and power for the later chapters. There is no need to completely master each section before moving to the next, but do not train solely for power if your mobility and stability are greatly lacking. This progression of exercises and chapters is easy to understand and easy to follow, and it is just as easy to achieve results in both your fitness and golf performance.

Achieving a body fit for golf will definitely reduce your risk of injury, but it can never guarantee an injury-free golf career. Since the golf swing is so explosive, injuries are bound to occur. For this specific reason, we have dedicated a chapter to the five body parts most commonly injured in golf. You will learn unique exercises for each body part that will help rehabilitate the area or avoid that specific injury. Knowing and understanding the most common injuries that can occur while you are playing golf can help you avoid putting yourself in a painful and sidelining situation.

With all this useful information, *Golf Anatomy* is truly written for a few different audiences. First and foremost, it is for any golfer who wants to avoid injury; improve fitness; and hit the ball farther, more accurately, and with more consistency. *Golf Anatomy* will help you understand the anatomy behind the swing and the tools to train that anatomy effectively. The second group that will benefit greatly from the information found in this book is teaching professionals. They will gain a much greater understanding of the body mechanics found within the swing. Instructors often are not aware of or are unable to identify inefficiencies or physical limitations in their students' bodies. This is due to no fault of their own as they are masters of the golf swing, not of the body. However, having a better grasp of the physical anatomy of a golfer's body can help teaching professionals give lessons with greater effectiveness, better understand how to avoid injuries in their golfers, and provide sound advice as to how to improve areas of dysfunction. The third group that can use this book to further their knowledge is strength and conditioning specialists. Although they are experts in fitness training, they might not have enough understanding of golf swing mechanics to apply the correct training protocols. *Golf Anatomy* provides this in-depth detail of the golf swing and will shed light on how training programs can be designed to effectively target the important aspects needed for an efficient and powerful swing.

# ACKNOWLEDGMENTS

This book was made possible through the unconditional encouragement, love, and support of the following people:

My wife and closest friend, Andrea. You have never wavered in your patience and belief in everything I have attempted and consequently achieved, both professionally and personally. My life is better for the major role you play in it.

My mom, sisters, and dad. Each of you has been my crutch at an important crossroad in my life. Your unwavering friendship and love is beyond measure.

Each of the players, at all levels of play, with whom I have worked. You have provided me the opportunity to share in your growth, dreams, and successes. I appreciate the passion, commitment, and belief you all have in yourselves and the trust you have in me. I am honored to be asked to help guide you on your travels.

All of my colleagues, teachers (especially my eighth-grade teacher, Ms. Barclay), and peers. You have challenged me professionally and personally and have encouraged me to dream large. I cannot thank you enough.

Sean Foley. Our many late-night talks on the patio, your refusal to be satisfied with the status quo, your passion for life, and your sage guidance are always a source of inspiration. You have been a positive force in my development on and off the course.

And finally, the game of golf and all those who love the long walk outdoors. Thank you for the experiences and opportunities!

**Craig Davies**


To my parents, who have always supported me and have made me who I am today; to my wife, who inspires me with her love and helps me navigate life's journey; and to my sons, who truly give my life purpose and make each day a blessing.

**Vince DiSaia**

# THE GOLFER IN MOTION

**P**icturing the world's best ball strikers conjures up images of effortless power and exceptional grace. Sergio Garcia, Alvaro Quiros, Rory McIlroy, and Geoff Ogilvy all seem to command the ball with power and balance. Picturing the average recreational golfer, perhaps one or all of your usual Saturday morning playing partners, often conjures up an image of a disjointed, uncoordinated movement that is at times complete chaos and futility. When a professional golfer hits balls, it seems like such an easy thing to do. However, the golf swing is one of the most complex movements in all of sport. Almost every joint and muscle in the body is utilized in some capacity during the golf swing. A weakness or deficiency in just one area can greatly reduce your ability to create an efficient swing. Lacking in more than one area can make generating and then transferring maximal force throughout the body extremely difficult if not altogether impossible.

One of the greatest misunderstandings of the average player, and sometimes even high-level players and golf coaches, is that speed and power in the golf swing is predominantly generated from the arms. This misunderstanding arose before high-speed video cameras, force plates, electromyography, and other types of expensive research equipment were used to measure forces and movements within the golf swing. In the prehistoric days of golf (any time before a few years ago), teachers and students could identify only what their eyes were able to see. Since the golf swing is such a quick movement, golfers were able to identify only the arm movement and the planes created by the arm and club. This thinking has drastically changed now that the golf swing has been analyzed and dissected using modern technology. You can't watch a PGA or LPGA event without having the commentators analyze a player's swing with the super-slow-motion bizhub camera. It is now evident that the arm and club actions are often a final thought in the actual development and execution of a golf swing.

A review of the driving distance statistics from the PGA Tour over several years reveals some interesting trends. Let's compare the number 1 player and number 50 player in terms of average driving distance for the years 1980, 1990, 2000, and 2008 (table 1.1). There were 20 players who averaged 299 yards or greater off the tee in 2008. The 50th player in terms of driving distance on tour in 2008 was hitting the ball farther than the 1st player in driving distance in 1996.

**Table 1.1  Average Distance for 1st and 50th Players in Driving Distance on PGA Tour**

| Year | 1st in driving distance | 50th in driving distance |
|------|-------------------------|--------------------------|
| 1980 | 274.3 yd | 261.0 yd |
| 1990 | 279.6 yd | 266.4 yd |
| 2000 | 301.4 yd | 277.5 yd |
| 2008 | 315.1 yd | 293.3 yd |

The recent increase in the distance off the tee can be attributed to many factors, the most obvious being improved ball, club-head, and shaft properties. Player fitness and the emergence of true athletes in golf's greatest tour, however, are also major contributors to this phenomenon. In the 1970s and even the 1980s, the number of true athletes on the professional golf tours was rather small when compared to today. The emergence of players such as Tiger Woods in the 1990s and increased purses made it more enticing for athletes to choose to pursue golf as an athletic career. If you look at the men on the PGA Tour these days, the transition of today's players from merely golfers to world-class athletes is obvious.

Although the women's tour has been much slower to adopt this emphasis on fitness, the change is occurring. Annika Sorenstam really pushed fitness in the women's game into the mid-2000s, and she dominated the game like no other member of the women's tour had. The many young stars of today's game, including the long-hitting Vicky Hurst, are incorporating fitness to help them achieve and maintain their success. Today's golfers at the high school, collegiate, and tour levels are bigger, faster, and stronger than they were in the past. The game has been forced to adapt to this new breed of golfer by instilling new rules on balls and clubs and making courses longer and more difficult. To keep up with these changes, golfers must continue to adapt themselves. This means maximizing their bodies to keep up with their peers. The recreational golfer is also affected by these changes. Many of today's new courses are being built longer in response to the turbo-charged play of today's top players. These changes in golf course architecture make it more difficult for the average player to compete. *Golf Anatomy* helps bridge that gap for the amateur by presenting an easy-to-follow manual for improving your golf fitness.

## Developing Proper Technique Through Golf Fitness

If there is one thing about golf that we have known for a long time, it is that proper technique is important. Swing coaches have been consulted for many years to help players dial in their swings with improved technique: correct grip, stance, takeaway, and so on. Coaches use an endless number of drills to help their golfers obtain certain feels and positions within the swing. However, the biggest revelation when it comes to the perfect way to swing a golf club is that there is no perfect way. A club can be swung an infinite number of ways. Many end with the same result—the club face hits the ball squarely at impact. The difference is the efficiency of the swing. If you put Hunter Mahan's swing next to Jim Furyk's swing, you would notice a huge difference. Obviously, both of these players are phenomenal golfers, and they are both considered world-class ball strikers. Although their swing styles look completely different, both have an efficient downswing that transfers a very high percentage of the energy produced during the downswing into the golf ball at impact. Comparing your swing with your favorite player's in an attempt to mimic his every movement often is not a sensible way to improve the technical side of your game. The key is to make your body capable of producing the most efficient swing that *you* can produce. The future of golf no longer relies solely on one standard swing to copy, but rather is a meshing of proper mechanical technique and efficiency of movement. Every player has an unique range of available motion in his joints, level of strength, and balance inconsistencies. Only by maximizing his own profile can a player truly achieve optimal competence.

One of the biggest problems that the common golfer encounters is the inability to achieve and reproduce positions that a swing coach desires. This is frustrating for both coach and student. Until recently, many people never considered that the golfer's body was the obstacle. If your car consistently drifts to the right when you are driving, you immediately suspect the alignment of your car needs a mechanical tune-up. It seems absurd we didn't think that a golfer who constantly moved in an undesirable direction might need a mechanical tune-up as well. In those prehistoric days, it was assumed that the golfer simply was not skilled enough to produce certain movements. So, the swing coach would have to work around those technical limitations.

Millions of dollars are spent each year on golf lessons in the United States alone. Even with this large monetary investment, the average North American handicap has not changed in the past 30 years. We must consider the fact that teaching of the golf swing has concentrated on changing only the aesthetic product (the movement) without developing the quality of the underlying machine, which can either enhance or inhibit the ability to create movement. Each joint in your body has a range of motion that is specific to you. Each of us is different. Some people have great mobility, and some are limited in their range of movement. If you can't rotate your shoulders through a full range of motion when you are at rest, how can they move through a full range of motion during the golf swing? It doesn't make sense to expect them to do so. The problem is, when learning to hit the ball better, many people try to move into positions that aren't physically possible because of limitations in range of motion. Not until the body improves to allow for greater range of motion and strength will a golfer be able to attain these positions during the golf swing.

This is why you need to achieve a certain level of golf fitness before expecting to make the desired swing changes properly and efficiently. The golf swing is, in fact, a very unnatural movement. You cannot expect your body to perform this task in the desired manner without the proper preparation.

So what is golf fitness, and how do you achieve it? Each sport has its own specific demands, and golf is no exception. However, golf fitness is much different from the fitness people go to the gym to achieve. We have all heard that golf is a game of opposites. This is no more evident than when you watch Anthony Kim or Andres Romero drive the ball more than 300 yards. How can someone with such a small frame crush the ball so far? Obviously it takes more than brute strength. Rather, it is the result of a perfect combination of a number of skill sets including, but not limited to, adequate mobility, stability, and balance. *Golf Anatomy* will show you not only which exercises are effective for producing an improved golf swing but also the order in which they should be performed.

The major characteristics that need to be trained for golf fitness are mobility, stability, balance, body awareness (proprioception), strength, and power. The order in which these specific components are trained is just as important as the components themselves. The correct progression of exercises provides the most efficient training and diminishes the risk of injury. Training for power before you have obtained an adequate amount of mobility increases the risk of injury and results in minimal golf-specific translation of fitness to the golf course. A solid foundation of mobility and stability is the essential building block for developing a body that is truly fit for the golf swing.

## Generating Power and Speed

At the sport's highest levels, it is increasingly common for players to adapt their swings for improved efficiency in power generation. Our goals in *Golf Anatomy* are to introduce exercises that will help you achieve greater golf fitness and introduce some of the important principles used by today's top teachers and players when developing a technically efficient golf swing.

Generating speed with the arms creates many of the swing faults found on driving ranges throughout North America and the world. For maximal power creation with minimal negative stress on the body, the ground must be the first link in the chain of energy transfer. Newton's third law of motion states that for every force applied by one object onto a second, an equal and opposite force is applied from the second object back onto the first. As such, using the legs to drive forcefully into the ground results in the ground pushing back up into the golfer's body with an equal magnitude of force. The force the ground transmits into the golfer is known as the ground reaction force (GRF). GRF is then transferred up through the legs and into the pelvis. From the pelvis the force is transferred into the golfer's core, shoulder complex, arms, and, finally, the golf club and ball. Transmitting this energy from the ground to the ball with the most efficiency is what allows you to create the most power your body will allow.

This energy moves through what is known as the body's kinetic chain. The different parts of the body act as a system of chain links, whereby the energy or force generated by one part of the body (or link) can be transferred successively to the next link. The optimal coordination (timing) of these body segments and their movements allows for the efficient transfer of energy and power up through the body, moving from one body segment to the next. Each movement in the sequence builds on the previous segment's motion and energy. The result of this transfer and summation is what determines club-head speed.

This kinetic chain is the linkage system that connects adjacent joints and muscles throughout the entire body. A weakness or injury in one area of the body impedes the transfer of energy. The body compensates for this blockage by overusing or misusing other body parts in an attempt to make up for this lost energy. In an efficient golf swing in which the legs generate the majority of the power, large muscles contribute to force generation. When a weakness is present along the body's kinetic chain, the energy produced by the legs is unable to transfer effectively into the core and arms. As a result, the smaller muscles surrounding the area of weakness are placed under great stress. In time, this will lead to overuse injuries within the joints and soft tissues (the muscles, tendons, and ligaments) and make an efficient swing impossible.

We must clarify what we mean by the word *weakness*. When referring to a weakness in the body's kinetic chain, we are not referring strictly to a lack of muscle strength. We also include deficits in joint motion and body awareness. Having proper ranges of motion in each of the body's segments and proper awareness of each of these segments is as important as the strength in each muscle. Therefore, weakness can mean a deficiency in strength, range of motion, or body awareness.

## Major Muscles and Joints Used During the Golf Swing

The golf swing involves nearly every muscle and joint in the body. As such, it is very difficult to pick just a few to highlight as the most important. For simplicity, we have attempted to highlight a variety of the major muscles and joints utilized during the various subsections of the full golf swing. This list is not all-encompassing but does provide a solid basis.

### Upswing, or Backswing

In general, the upswing phase (figure 1.1), also known as the backswing, is performed with much less tension and physical stress throughout the body than the remainder of the golf swing. In this phase, balance, proprioception, and joint and muscle mobility are often more important than actual muscle strength. Having sufficient external rotation and retraction of the trail-side shoulder complex (the right shoulder in a right-handed golfer) and abduction, internal rotation, and protraction on the target side (the left shoulder in a right-handed golfer) while also possessing sufficient internal rotation of the trail hip, external rotation of the target hip, and spinal rotation is more important than how strong the big muscle groups are. The problem with many golfers' fitness programs is a lack of time spent on increasing mobility or flexibility. If a golfer is restricted in his ability to move his body into a desirable position while remaining in balance during the upswing, the remainder of the golf swing is negatively affected regardless of the muscular strength or explosiveness of that athlete.

Although this phase of the swing uses mostly a golfer's mobility, some muscles provide a stable base so others can maximize their movements. During the upswing, the golfer must load the quadriceps, gluteus medius, and gluteus maximus in the trail leg and the obliques as the golfer coils toward the

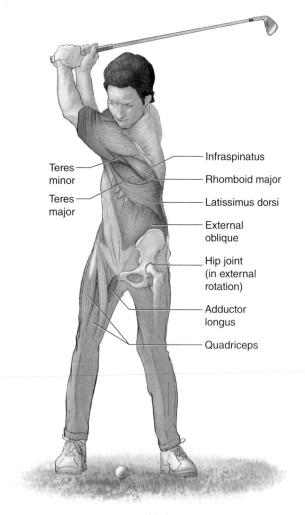

Teres minor

Teres major

Infraspinatus

Rhomboid major

Latissimus dorsi

External oblique

Hip joint (in external rotation)

Adductor longus

Quadriceps

Figure 1.1   Muscles used during the upswing phase.

top of this phase of the golf swing. When these muscles work efficiently, the latissimus dorsi, infraspinatus, rhomboids, obliques, and multifidi can elongate properly to achieve the correct, full position of the upswing.

A great deal of time during golf lessons is spent attempting to attain positions in the backswing. Average and even high-level golfers spend very little time on the downswing or follow-through. During fitness training, most golfers do work on developing adequate motion throughout their bodies. However, many golfers may be unable to properly achieve the positions the golf professional wants. When positive changes are not seen, the result is frustration for both players and professionals and may lead to injury and poor performance. When golfers increase their mobility to match the motion the instructor is trying to get them to create during the upswing, more time can be spent learning the downswing, impact, and follow-through phases of the swing.

## Downswing

The transition from the upswing to the downswing (figure 1.2) requires great coordination by the athlete and an ability to separate the lower body and pelvis from the upper body. The transition between these two phases of the swing is initiated by the golfer moving the lower body into position to allow for the greatest muscular efficiency. One of the primary objectives is to position the target-side knee over the outside aspect of the target foot. This puts the golfer in proper alignment for the quadriceps muscles to contract and straighten the knee, the gluteus maximus muscle to contract to create hip extension, and the muscles of the hip rotator cuff (piriformis, gluteus medius and minimus, and obturators) to contract to create both lateral stability within the hip and internal rotation of the hip joint, all on the target-side leg. The trail-side leg uses the quadriceps, adductor magnus, hamstrings, gluteus maximus, and gastrocnemius muscles to create knee extension, hip extension, and ankle plantar flexion to help drive the golfer's weight onto the left side. The activation of the muscles in the legs helps drive the golfer into the ground and position the player so that the arms are able to move into position and create the desired angles of attack.

In the core, the obliques and psoas major are highly activated, creating a crunch-like position as the golfer's hips extend and his pelvis tilts in a relatively posterior fashion (the belt buckle starts to point up) while his chest remains over the ball. The target-side latissimus dorsi helps pull the golfer onto his target side while countering the force generated by the pectoralis muscles on both sides of the golfer's body.

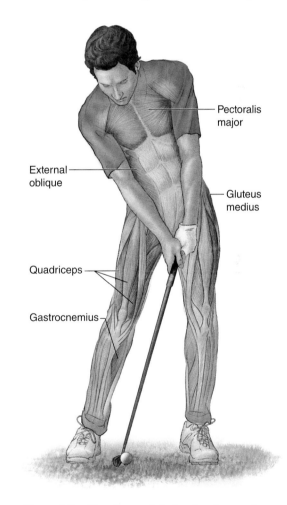

Figure 1.2   Muscles used during the downswing.

## Follow-Through

The follow-through movement in the golf swing (figure 1.3) allows for deceleration of the body, specifically the arms, post-impact. This phase of the golf swing is very taxing because the muscles must work predominantly through eccentric contractions to slow down the body. The golfer's entire core—obliques, quadratus lumborum, psoas major, and transversus and rectus abdominis—works at maximum power to produce force and decelerate the body. The latissimus dorsi and the muscles that stabilize the shoulder blade to the spine and rib cage (serratus anterior, rhomboids, levator scapulae) as well as the muscles of the rotator cuff (supraspinatus, infraspinatus, teres minor, subscapularis) help protect the shoulder joint from approaching its end range of motion under high velocity.

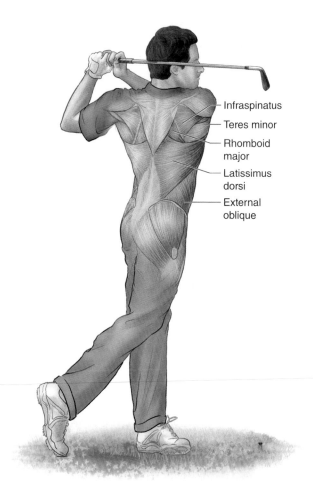

Infraspinatus

Teres minor

Rhomboid major

Latissimus dorsi

External oblique

Figure 1.3   Muscles used during the follow-through.

## Understanding Body Awareness

Often body awareness, or proprioception, is the most overlooked sense. It is as important as the other senses for optimal athletic functioning, if not more important. Proprioception is the process by which the body can use muscles in immediate response to its surroundings. Your body must be able to respond rapidly to changing body positions and different forces throughout the swing. Imagine how many body parts are moving in different directions during the golf swing, all in less than three seconds from the initiation of the upswing to the end of the follow-through. How can your body keep up with all that information? The body is able to do this through tiny receptors in the muscles and joints that keep track of every joint position in the body. The better these receptors work with their respective muscles, the better body awareness you will have throughout the entire golf swing. This will greatly help you produce the correct movements and angles necessary for a good swing more frequently.

Kinesthesia is the ability to sense joint motion and acceleration. Proprioception and kinesthesia are the sensory feedback mechanisms for motor control and posture. These mechanisms help orient the body and maintain balance and are unconsciously utilized by the brain and spinal reflexes to provide a constant influx of sensory information. The central nervous system (brain and spinal cord) translates this sensory information and sends out immediate and unconscious adjustments to the muscles and joints in order to achieve specific movement and balance.

Your ability to balance under different circumstances depends on how well your body senses changes to body position and the forces applied against and within it. Walking, riding an escalator, and treading on uneven ground are some examples in which the body requires proprioceptive input to maintain balance during motion.

Just as training can lead to increases in muscular strength, training can also increase the accuracy and speed with which the body is able to perceive and respond to various positions and forces. Because improvements in balance and proprioception come through neural adaptation and often do not require an actual increase in muscle mass, these are often the quickest skill sets to improve once they are consciously incorporated into a fitness program.

## Transferring Power

When a right-handed golfer initiates the downswing, he shifts his body weight onto his target side (left side) by positioning his target-side knee (left knee) over his target-side foot (left foot). This places the golfer's lower body into an ideal force-generating position. With the knee over the foot, the quadriceps can function to straighten the knee, and the gluteus maximus and hamstring muscles can contract to create extension of the hip and pelvis. This combined extension movement drives the target foot into the ground. The ground creates a resultant force back into the golfer that can be passed effortlessly through the legs and into the golfer's pelvis and core. If the pelvis and core are functionally strong and are able to move through the desired range of motion, the force will pass into the shoulder complex. The shoulder complex consists of the muscles connecting the spine and ribs to the shoulder blade and the muscles connecting the shoulder blade to the arm. If the shoulder complex is functioning optimally, this force can be transferred into the arms and, finally, into compression of the golf ball.

In addition, using the legs to position the golfer and create power helps minimize an over-the-top, slice-generating swing. The lateral shift of the lower body onto the target side brings the plane of the downswing forward toward the target. As such, the arc of the club will automatically have a more inside swing path.

When a golfer initiates the golf swing with her upper body, the angular momentum of the golf club forces the club head out away from the body on the downswing. Once initiated, this angular momentum provides resistance through inertia against the golfer's body, preventing the body from moving forward toward the target. Visually, you see a golfer who appears to have fast hips. It appears her hips are rotating too quickly, which forces the club out and away from the body as the trail shoulder moves forward toward the ball, creating an over-the-top, slice-generating swing plane. Often a player like this is told to slow down the hips. Actually, the problem is not that her hips are turning too fast but that she is using her arms to generate the power and not using her legs to shift forward toward the target. When this player learns to use her legs to push into the ground, her apparently fast-rotating hips will appear to slow automatically, and her club head will begin to attack the ball from the inside more easily.

Players who appear to have fast hips and have trouble attacking the ball from the inside are rotating predominately through the joints in the lower back with minimal rotation actually occurring at the hip joint. This lower-back-centered movement is especially stressful on the spine and supporting muscles. The wear and tear eventually will lead to pain.

## Training for Success

How can so many of today's top players, such as Hunter Mahan, Anthony Kim, and Sean O'Hair, combine power and finesse in their golf swings? Part of the answer is obvious—their technique is world class. The other part of the answer is not as obvious. They are able to move each part of their bodies through the required range of motion while simultaneously maintaining kinetic balance, stability, and power. When one of these skill sets is limited, a golfer's efficiency in transferring energy is diminished, the golf swing suffers, and injuries occur. For this reason, each of these players puts a lot of time and effort into ensuring his body is in functionally optimal form. This includes daily sessions in the PGA fitness trailers during tournament weeks, regular treatment sessions—both for injury prevention and injury maintenance—and aggressive off-week fitness regimens.

Each week, these players include various forms of fitness in their routines: mobility exercises like those found in yoga, stability movements for the core and shoulder regions, balance and proprioception exercises, and strength and power movements. They use exercise equipment such as tubing and cables, medicine balls, stability balls, traditional weights, cardio equipment, and kettlebells. Many exercises require only body weight. It is important to use more than one type of training methodology in your golf fitness program to ensure a constant and progressive challenge to your body. In many aspects of life, people tend to practice what they are good at and ignore what they find challenging or difficult. Often decent ball strikers spend the majority of their practice time beating balls on the range and almost completely ignore their short-game practice. The same occurs in the gym: People work on their strengths and ignore their weaknesses. For example, athletes who have poor flexibility often ignore or invest minimal time on a mobility program and spend the majority of their time executing traditional strength training exercises. This behavior leads to minimal carryover of the gains attained in the gym onto the golf course. The end result is frustration and a lot of wasted time.

Whether you are one of the golf world's up-and-coming stars like Danny Lee or Jamie Lovemark, an established veteran like Stephen Ames, Lorena Ochoa, or Robert Allenby, or an amateur player looking to improve your game for future club rounds, using your time efficiently is important. We all wish we had more time to do the things we love. Unfortunately, our time is limited, and we need to maximize the time we do have. The exercises in this book have been chosen to maximize efficiency so that you see results both on the course and in your daily life in a short period of time.

*Golf Anatomy* has also been developed to help you avoid the common pitfalls of fitness training of all types. Remember, there are different skill sets involved in developing fitness. Often athletes want to move directly from minimal or no specific fitness training to the most difficult or complicated movements. This methodology often leads to poor long-term performance gains and increased likelihood of injury and mechanical restrictions. It is important to develop good balance, mobility, stability, and basic strength before attempting the power movements found in this book, in magazines, and on the Web. If you listen to your body and gradually progress through your exercise prescription, you should see great improvements while staying safe and free of injury.

Many of the legends of golf incurred problems with injuries toward the ends of their careers. Jack Nicklaus, Arnold Palmer, and Tom Watson all required hip reconstruction. Fred Couples and Tommy Armour III have had significant problems with their backs. Tiger Woods has significant knee problems that may challenge his ability to win a record number of majors. Trevor Immelman, Phil Mickelson, and Michelle Wie have been sidelined with wrist injuries. Injuries plague the golf world at a staggering level. It is not uncommon to see members of any golf foursome, regardless of age or skill level, use some form of pain modulator either before or after a round of golf. Many injuries that require the use of pain medication occurred off the course but limit the player's ability to play pain free on the course. The injury chapter of *Golf Anatomy* has a variety of low-stress exercises that are useful for golfers suffering from an injury. This chapter is divided into sections that provide specific exercise movements to help the most commonly injured areas within a golfer's body. These exercises are also great choices for anyone who has limited experience in fitness training because they are low impact and most require minimal experience.

The goal of *Golf Anatomy* is to give you the basics to develop a golf fitness program that is specific to your needs. We encourage you to seek the help of a golf fitness professional in incorporating these movements into your current program. Golf is a wonderful activity that can contribute to a healthy lifestyle through encouraging both increased physical activity and social interaction. *Golf Anatomy* will help increase your enjoyment on the course through improved functional capabilities and a decreased likelihood of on-course injury and discomfort.

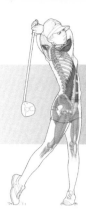

# CHAPTER 2

# MOBILITY FOR OPTIMAL SWING ANGLES

The golf swing is a multiplane, multidirectional movement that requires most of the body's joints to perform through near-maximal ranges of motion. When a joint or muscle is limited in its available motion, a number of negative repercussions occur. Some of these negative results include poor performance, increased potential for injury, and less enjoyment of the game. On the contrary, adequate mobility not only helps prevent injuries but also provides a foundation on which consistency, accuracy, and power can be built.

As mentioned in chapter 1, the ability to generate consistency and efficiency in the golf swing is dependent on a number of distinct physical abilities and skill sets. These include mobility, stability, strength, power, endurance, balance, and body awareness. When a golfer is lacking in any of these, the golf swing will be partially compromised. The more severe the skill-set deficit, the more serious the negative effect.

One of the more common misconceptions in golf is how distance is achieved off the tee and from the fairway. Many people believe that increasing a golfer's strength alone will result in greater distance with the driver. This idea is based on poor understanding of the body mechanics, physics, and techniques used by elite-level golfers. If the most important factor for hitting long drives were how much a golfer can bench press or squat, every running back who picked up a golf club would hit the ball a mile. We all know this isn't true. Many of the long-distance hitters on the PGA Tour do not have excessively overdeveloped muscles or look like your typical bodybuilder. Sean O'Hair and Dustin Johnson are great examples of lean players who consistently hit the ball more than 300 yards. Conversely, John Daly made a career of hitting monster golf shots, and he probably didn't make it into the gym very often, if at all.

The body's ability to create specific angles and motions throughout the golf swing has more impact on producing high club-head speed than one's ability to lift big weights. Mobility plays a central role in golf, not only in achieving longer distance but also in improving accuracy, improving consistency, and avoiding injury. The one thing that Sean O'Hair, Dustin Johnson, and John Daly share with Tiger Woods, besides having the ability to hit the ball forever, is great mobility. Golfers who have above-average mobility throughout their bodies can often have great golf swings even if they are lacking in one of the other core skill sets we describe in this book.

Having said that, if two golfers are able to create the same angles throughout the golf swing, the one who has the most functional strength (this is different from traditional bodybuilding strength) would have an edge in distance in most cases. This chapter, and the entire book, will help you create both the angles needed in a good golf swing and the functional strength to become efficient and powerful.

Any golfer who has taken a golf lesson has experienced the frustration of not being able to move his body and club into the positions his teacher wants him to achieve. This inability to follow instruction is usually not from lack of desire but is often a direct result of mobility issues within the player's body. When a golfer has limitations in his ability to move his joints and muscles through full ranges of motion, he will not be able to position himself to create proper angles. This, of course, is to the dissatisfaction of the golf instructor and the irritation of the student.

When any area of the body is compromised in its ability to function through the desired range with satisfactory strength, the body will compensate by attempting to make up this lost movement at another area of the body. An example of this is the lower back rotating excessively to compensate for a loss of (internal) rotation at the hips. This compensatory motion within the lower back usually results in both decreased performance (an over-the-top swing path is often seen) and increased likelihood of injury to the lower back.

The two main goals of all avid golfers should be (1) to play this wonderful game in a manner that will allow pain-free play for as long as they want, regardless of age, and (2) to reach their full potential in terms of level of play. For these two goals to be achieved, a player's golf swing cannot be allowed to cause injury. For this reason, sufficient mobility is the basic building block that must be addressed when attempting to play golf at any level (figure 2.1).

When golfers attend our testing facilities, regardless

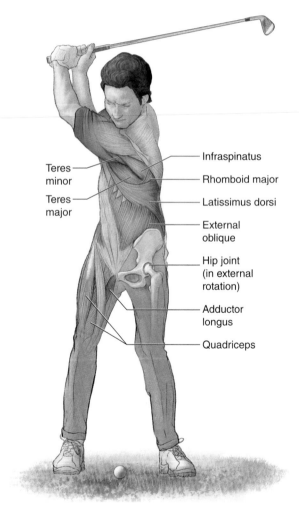

Teres minor

Teres major

Infraspinatus

Rhomboid major

Latissimus dorsi

External oblique

Hip joint (in external rotation)

Adductor longus

Quadriceps

**Figure 2.1**  Excellent mobility enables the golfer to create the proper angles during the swing.

of whether they are PGA Tour or amateur-level players, we are always able to find areas within the players' bodies that have limited ranges of functional motion. These limitations often result in the players creating compensatory movements in their golf swing that lead to reactive stress in adjacent muscles and joints. This happens because the body is attempting to make up for the motion lost within the area of restriction. For those players playing at the highest level of professional golf, a restriction in body function can lead to both huge financial losses and injury. It is common for professional golfers to visit our facilities as a last resort because they have been unable to resolve inefficiencies in their swing with their golf instructors. If a player has put a significant amount of time and effort into making a technical change to his golf swing but has had limited success, the most common contributor is physical limitations in his mobility. Quite often we will find a limitation in a golfer's movements during testing that has a direct correlation to his inability to make a specific swing change. Once the golfer corrects the movement deficiency, the swing changes can be made easily and successfully.

Although increasing mobility is important, traditional stretching has not been shown to be very effective for improving golf performance. The reason for these limited improvements is that the golf swing requires the body to move through ranges of motion not seen in normal daily activities. It is important that golfers practice movements specific to those required in the golf swing in order to achieve the desired golf-specific flexibility. To do this, it is also important to learn how to stretch muscles in combination and not just in isolation.

We have written this chapter to educate the average player about movements that will not only improve the ranges of motion desired for the golf swing but also increase the functional strength within the entire range of motion. As you read through the exercises outlined in this chapter, you will notice that the movements described are not the traditional stretches most of us have learned from books, videos, or gym classes. Most of the flexibility exercises require you to move while lengthening the muscles and associated soft tissues (tendons, ligaments, and joint capsules). We have found that this is the most effective way to improve joint and muscle mobility for sport-specific purposes.

Perform 8 to 15 repetitions of the exercises in this chapter unless otherwise stated. For exercises you find easy to perform, complete all 15 repetitions. For exercises you find difficult to perform while maintaining proper form, complete only as many repetitions as you can with correct form, even if you complete fewer than 8. Complete 3 sets of each exercise, regardless of how many repetitions you do. Since these exercise focus on mobility, it is more important to complete more repetitions with a full range of motion than it is to increase weight (if you are using weights) and reduce the number of repetitions.

# Cats and Dogs

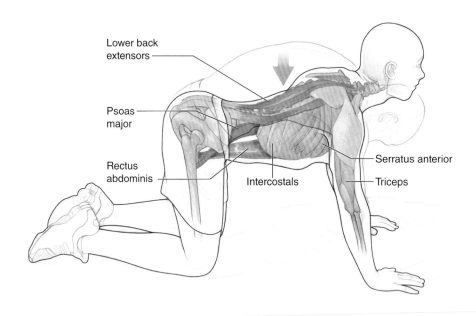

Lower back extensors

Psoas major

Rectus abdominis

Intercostals

Serratus anterior

Triceps

## Execution

1. Begin on all fours with knees under hips, hands under shoulders, and arms slightly bent.
2. Keep your head and neck in a straight line with your spine.
3. Pull your belly button to your spine, round your back up as high as you can, and tuck your chin in toward your chest.
4. Squeeze your shoulder blades together, arch your back down toward the floor, and lift your head until you're looking forward.
5. Return to start position and repeat.

## Muscles Involved

**Primary:** Lower back extensors, psoas major, rectus abdominis

**Secondary:** Triceps, serratus anterior, intercostals

## Golf Focus

A common problem for the average player is a lack of mobility in the spine and pelvis. Players who have poor spinal mobility often appear to be slumped and rounded forward in the shoulders and lower back. These postural issues make it difficult to create a straighter spine at setup. What most golfers don't realize is that poor spinal posture affects the golf swing more than you would think. When the spine is not able to move forward (flexion) and backward (extension) easily, it has a negative influence on the mobility of the shoulder blades and pelvis through the muscle connections between the spine and these body areas. When the hips and pelvis become

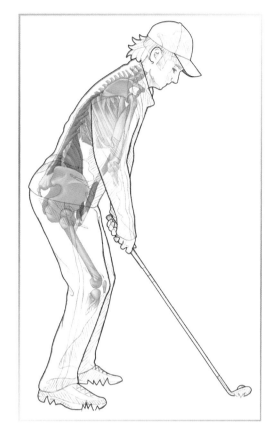

limited in their range of motion, the potential for injury is greatly increased, and the likelihood of improving the swing technique is greatly reduced. Cats and dogs is a great initial exercise to help promote proper spinal mobility.

# Golf Posture Posterior Pelvic Tilt

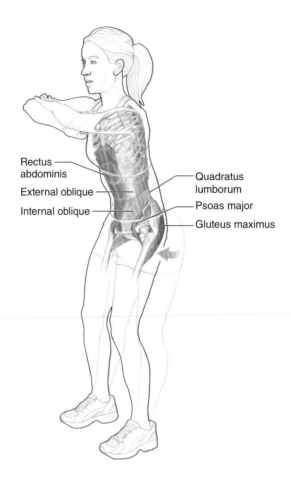

Rectus abdominis

External oblique

Internal oblique

Quadratus lumborum

Psoas major

Gluteus maximus

## Execution

1. Stand with feet hip-width apart.
2. Hinge at the hips into your 7-iron posture.
3. Bend and cross your arms in front of you.
4. Pull your belly button back toward your spine as you tilt or curl your tailbone under your pelvis. Do not let your shoulders move during the exercise.
5. Return to start position.

## Muscles Involved

**Primary:** Lower back extensors, rectus abdominis, gluteus maximus, psoas major

**Secondary:** Internal oblique, external oblique, quadratus lumborum

## Golf Focus

It is very important for a golfer to learn how to move the pelvis into extension, flexion, and neutral postures. This is important in preventing back pain and to allow for proper weight transfer to the lead leg at impact and follow-through. Many golfers have a tendency to be stuck in an anterior tilt of the pelvis. In this position there is too much curve in the lower back (known as hyperlordosis). This position places greater stress on the joints in the lower back, and there is often an association with trail-side lower back tightness or pain. Learning how to position your pelvis properly will allow you to keep your spine in a safer posture throughout the golf swing and allow for better weight transfer to the lead leg (left leg in a right-handed golfer).

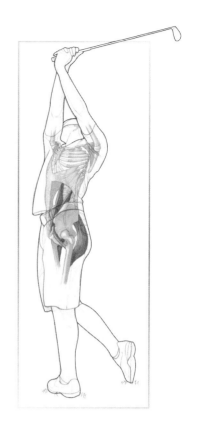

## VARIATION

### Pelvic Tilt on Back

To make this exercise easier, you can perform the pelvic tilt while lying on your back. Your hips and knees should both be bent to approximately 45 degrees. As you exhale, your abdomen should come toward your back, and your lower back will flatten. Inhale and let your back return to a slight arch.

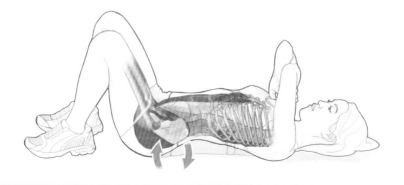

# Cobra

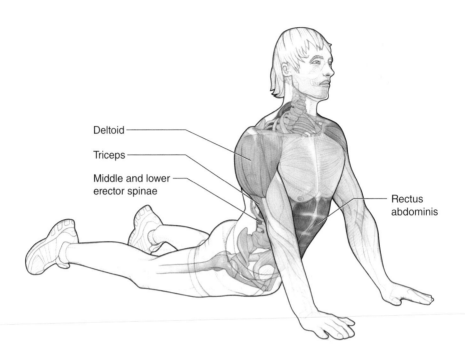

Deltoid

Triceps

Middle and lower
erector spinae

Rectus
abdominis

## Execution

1. Lie on your abdomen with your forehead resting on your forearms.
2. Trying to keep your pelvis on the floor, look straight ahead, slowly push yourself up onto your hands, and try to get your chest as vertical as possible.
3. Hold for a few seconds, slowly return to the start position, and repeat.

## Muscles Involved

**Primary:** Middle and lower erector spinae, rectus abdominis

**Secondary:** Deltoid, triceps

## Golf Focus

This exercise must be performed within tolerance. Never attempt to press up beyond your ability or to the point of pain. Assuming you can perform this exercise without pain, it becomes important for keeping the spine mobile and helping to reduce stiffness in the lower and middle back. This mobility is crucial to the golfer, not only to maintain proper upright posture throughout the swing but also to allow the body to move smoothly through all rotational ranges of motion. Developing stiffness in the lower back or

rounding of the middle back will reduce the ability to rotate properly and will alter proper swing mechanics. This ultimately leads to faulty swing patterns and increased risk of injury.

### VARIATION

### Modified Cobra

If the full version of the cobra either causes pain or cannot be done because of limited mobility in your spine, then perform the same exercise but push up onto your forearms. This requires less spinal motion and will be easier to perform.

# Pelvic Thrust on Stability Ball

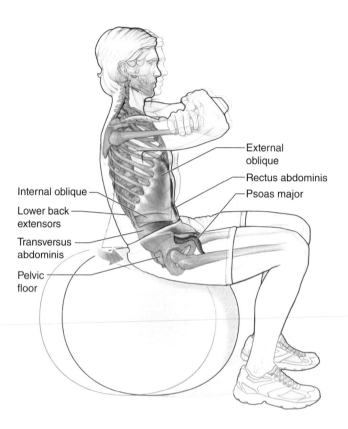

External oblique

Rectus abdominis

Internal oblique

Psoas major

Lower back extensors

Transversus abdominis

Pelvic floor

## Execution

1. Sit on a stability ball with your chest up and shoulders back, and your lower back in a neutral position.
2. Flatten your lower back by sliding the hips forward (the ball should move slightly forward).
3. Slowly arch your lower back as you slide your hips back under you (the ball should move slightly backward). Keep the chest up and shoulders back throughout the exercise—do not slouch.
4. Return to neutral and repeat.

## Muscles Involved

**Primary:** Rectus abdominis, transversus abdominis, psoas major

**Secondary:** External oblique, internal oblique, pelvic floor, lower back extensors

## Golf Focus

As mentioned in the first couple of exercises, it is very important for a golfer to be able to set up to the ball with a neutral spinal posture. The chest should be up and the shoulders back. There should not be a rounding of the upper back or excessive extension in the lower back. The joints in the spine should be positioned in a manner that allows the greatest amount of rotation when they are aligned in a neutral position (not slumped forward or extended backward). Being able to create a neutral position in the spine allows you to rotate into your backswing, downswing, and follow-through phases easier, with greater movement and less stress on the body. This is an easy but important exercise to perform and master. When this becomes too easy, try the variation. The pelvic thrust and figure 8 exercises provide a safe and controlled means of learning how to move the pelvis for improved posture.

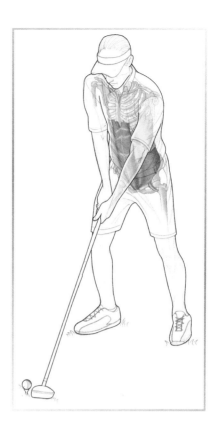

## VARIATION

### Figure 8 on Stability Ball

The figure 8 works the same musculature but requires you to control precise movements of the pelvis. As your pelvis moves in a figure 8, your shoulders should not move much and should be pulled back the entire exercise. Perform in both side-to-side and forward-to-backward motions.

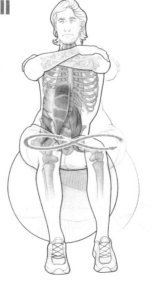

# Dynamic Child's Pose

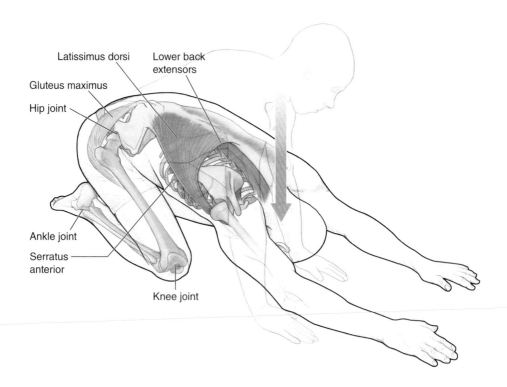

Latissimus dorsi

Lower back extensors

Gluteus maximus

Hip joint

Ankle joint

Serratus anterior

Knee joint

## Execution

1. Kneel on the ground, sit on top of your heels, and keep your back straight.
2. Slowly bend forward at the waist, touch your forehead to the ground, and reach as far in front of you as possible.
3. Remain in that stretched position for a few moments, return to the start position, and repeat.

## Muscles Involved

**Primary:** Latissimus dorsi, lower back extensors, serratus anterior

**Secondary:** Gluteus maximus, intercostals, tibialis anterior

## Golf Focus

Correct swing planes are very important for a consistent and efficient golf swing. If your body does not allow you to move freely, then achieving the proper path of the club will be very difficult. Your body responds by finding other ways to move the club through the backswing and downswing, which will greatly reduce efficiency. Shoulder and latissimus dorsi ranges of motion are critical for a correct swing. If either is limited, then the club will be out of position at the top of the backswing, causing compensations within the downswing. Touring professionals might be able to compensate enough to hit a good shot, 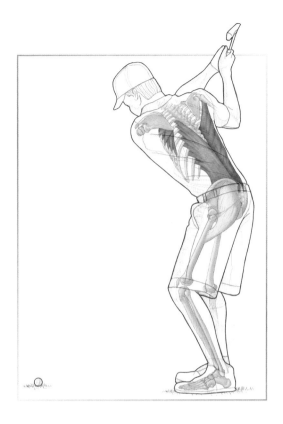 but this lack of movement will certainly cause loss of power, inefficient swing mechanics, inconsistent ball striking, and potential for injury. For the average golfer, these limitations can make it very difficult to hit the ball straight because each downswing begins on an incorrect path. The dynamic child's pose will help increase mobility in the shoulders and surrounding musculature so that your body is ready to swing the club on the correct path.

The dynamic child's pose also will help you achieve greater flexibility of the ligaments, joint capsules, and muscles at the hip, knee, and ankle, which many golfers find beneficial on and off the golf course.

## VARIATION

### Standing Side Bend With Overhead Reach

The standing side bend allows you to work the latissimus dorsi and the serratus anterior without putting any pressure on the joints of your lower body. Stand with feet slightly wider than shoulder-width apart. Lean your upper body to the left while reaching your right arm overhead toward the left. Repeat with the other arm.

# Heel Touch

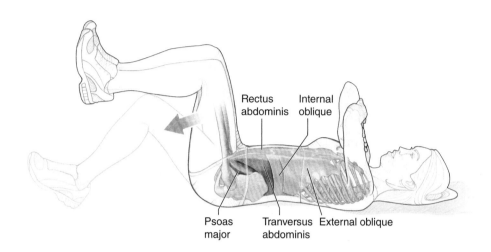

Rectus abdominis    Internal oblique

Psoas major    Tranversus abdominis    External oblique

## Execution

1. Lie on your back with both legs in the air. Hips and knees should be bent to 90 degrees.
2. Keeping your knee bent 90 degrees, slowly lower your left leg until your heel touches the ground. Do not allow your lower back to move.
3. Return to the start position and repeat with the opposite leg.

## Muscles Involved

**Primary:** Psoas major, transversus abdominis

**Secondary:** External oblique, internal oblique, rectus abdominis

## Golf Focus

When you address the golf ball, proper positioning is key for setting up the correct swing path. The muscles used to perform heel touches will help prepare your body for the right address position. These muscles, which are used to hold your pelvis and lower spine in the address position, also become very important throughout the swing. If you do not have both the mobility and strength to maintain this position, then the forces of the golf swing will certainly cause you to lose your posture. This exercise will help you increase your ability to maintain proper lower back and pelvic angles, both at address and throughout the entire swing. The importance of this is twofold: First, correct pelvis and lower torso posture allows the body to rotate with much greater efficiency. Second, moving through the golf swing while maintaining proper angles greatly reduces the forces, and therefore the stresses, applied to various joints and muscles.

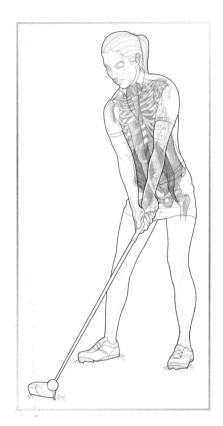

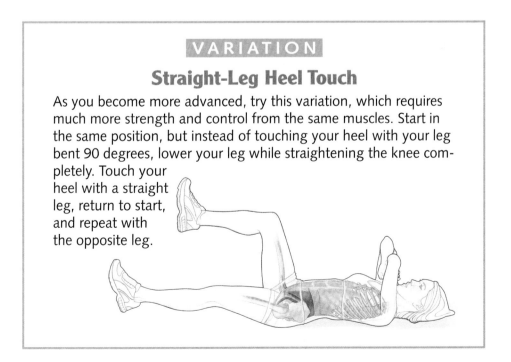

### VARIATION

### Straight-Leg Heel Touch

As you become more advanced, try this variation, which requires much more strength and control from the same muscles. Start in the same position, but instead of touching your heel with your leg bent 90 degrees, lower your leg while straightening the knee completely. Touch your heel with a straight leg, return to start, and repeat with the opposite leg.

# Wall Angel

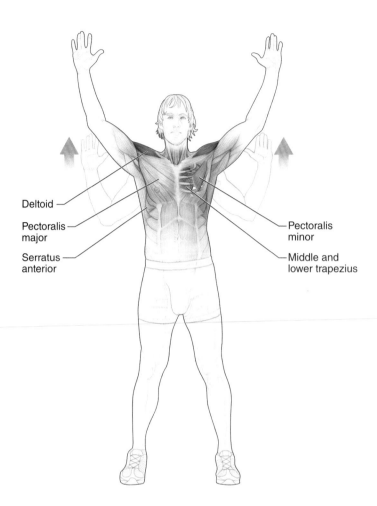

Deltoid

Pectoralis major

Serratus anterior

Pectoralis minor

Middle and lower trapezius

## Execution

1. Stand with your back and head flat against a wall, knees bent, and feet 12 inches (30 cm) from the wall.
2. Bend your elbows, and place the elbows and wrists flat against the wall.
3. While keeping your back and head against the wall, slowly raise your arms up the wall without letting your elbows or wrists come off the wall.
4. Return your arms to the start position and repeat.

## Muscles Involved

**Primary:** Deltoid, middle trapezius, lower trapezius

**Secondary:** Pectoralis major, pectoralis minor, serratus anterior

## Golf Focus

The movements of the golf swing require certain parts of the body to stabilize while others are moving. Your arms need to move through a large range of motion with every golf swing. This must be done with relative stability of the torso. If your upper back tends to round excessively forward, then shoulder movement will be restricted and swing faults will develop. Wall angels help train the mobility and strength of the shoulders while the spine stays stable and in an upright position. This mimics the requirements of the golf swing, where proper upper body posture allows for not only optimal shoulder movement but also improved rotation throughout the spine during the entire swing. Once this exercise can be achieved freely and without excessive strain, you will find that obtaining appropriate angles within the swing becomes much easier to achieve. Ultimately, this leads to better and more consistent ball striking as well as decreased injury risk.

---

### VARIATION

## Supine Wall Angel

If wall angels prove to be too difficult for you, then do the same exercise on your back with your knees slightly bent and feet against the floor. This takes gravity out of the equation, making the exercise slightly easier.

# Pelvic Disassociation

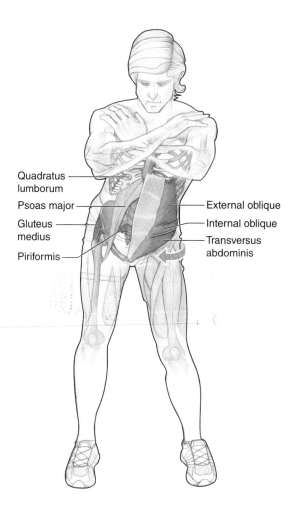

Quadratus lumborum

Psoas major

Gluteus medius

Piriformis

External oblique

Internal oblique

Transversus abdominis

## Execution

1. Start in your 7-iron golf posture with your arms crossed in front of your chest.
2. Without moving your shoulders or chest, slowly turn your pelvis and hips to the right.
3. Return your pelvis to midline, and repeat to the left.
4. Try this exercise in front of a mirror to make sure your shoulders and chest do not move with your pelvis and hips.

## Muscles Involved

**Primary:** Transversus abdominis, internal oblique, external oblique, gluteus medius, piriformis

**Secondary:** Psoas major, lower back extensors, quadratus lumborum

## Golf Focus

The ability to properly separate the pelvis from the shoulders is an important skill to have. When the pelvis is able to separate from the shoulders at the onset of the downswing and move toward the target, you are able to generate more coil through the core. This creates the potential for greater power on the downswing and greater club-head speed at impact. When a golfer is unable to separate her pelvis from her shoulders, she will rotate her whole body at the same time during her golf swing and will have an over-the-top or out-to-in swing path with her arms and club. She will also have less speed through the ball. This leads to less distance with every club and quite often a slice ball path. The pelvic disassociation exercise will teach you how to move the pelvis independently of the shoulders. When you can do this easily and have done the disassociation strengthening exercises found in this chapter, you will possess the physical attributes to both create and close the separation of the pelvis and shoulder (the so-called X factor).

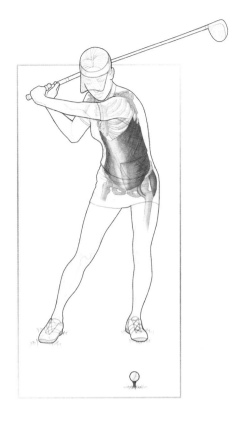

### VARIATION

## Core Disassociation

This variation will also improve your disassociation, but this time you will be keeping your pelvis and hips still while you move your torso. Make sure that you keep your lower body completely still, and allow your torso to rotate both ways while remaining in golf posture as much as possible.

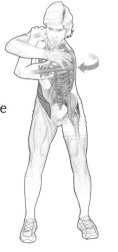

# Dynamic Latissimus

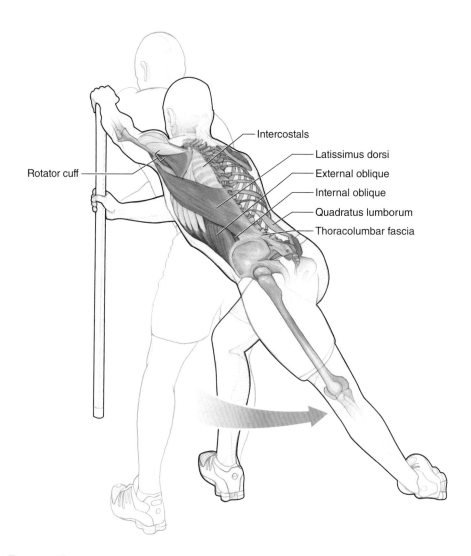

Intercostals

Latissimus dorsi

Rotator cuff

External oblique

Internal oblique

Quadratus lumborum

Thoracolumbar fascia

## Execution

1. Stand 2 feet (.6 m) away from a pole.
2. Grab the pole with a straight left arm, and turn your body until your breastbone is facing your left elbow.
3. Bend your knees and push your rib cage to the left. Feel a slight pull along your left-side ribs.
4. Straighten your left leg behind your bent right leg.
5. The left leg and arm form a U around your right leg.
6. Hold for 20 seconds and repeat on the right side. Perform 3 or 4 times on each side.

## Muscles Involved

**Primary:** Latissimus dorsi, internal oblique, external oblique, rotator cuff

**Secondary:** Thoracolumbar fascia, quadratus lumborum, intercostals

## Golf Focus

It is very important to create mobility within the connections (fascia) that join the lead arm (left arm in a right-handed golfer), the big latissimus dorsi muscles (the wings on bodybuilders), the lower back, and the gluteus muscles. This allows the golfer to maintain a straight lead arm while making a full shoulder turn into the top of the backswing and through the downswing. The dynamic latissimus is a great exercise movement to help increase the length of this area of the body and increase the perceived ease of shoulder turn at the top of the swing.

## VARIATION

### Dynamic Latissimus With Golf Cart

To help keep your core and shoulders loose on the golf course, do the same stretch by holding onto one of the poles of your golf cart. This will allow you to keep this muscle loose while playing so that tight muscles do not affect your swing toward the end of the round.

# Trunk Rotation on Stability Ball

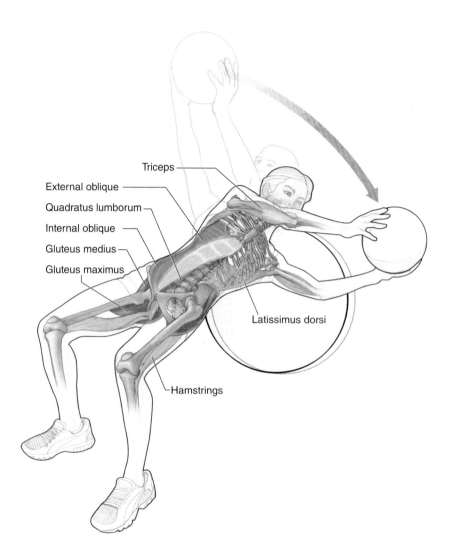

Triceps

External oblique

Quadratus lumborum

Internal oblique

Gluteus medius

Gluteus maximus

Latissimus dorsi

Hamstrings

## Execution

1. Lie with your head and shoulders on a stability ball. Push your hips up in line with your knees and shoulders.
2. Hold a medicine ball with straight arms above your chest.
3. Rotate your upper body and arms together to the left 90 degrees. Your left shoulder should now be on the stability ball, and your right shoulder should face the ceiling.
4. During left rotation, the stability ball will move slightly to the right.
5. Return to the start position and repeat to the right.

## Muscles Involved

**Primary:** Gluteus medius, gluteus maximus, internal oblique, external oblique

**Secondary:** Latissimus dorsi, quadratus lumborum, triceps, hamstrings

## Golf Focus

As we mentioned previously, the ability to create separation between the pelvis and the shoulders is an important factor in producing potential energy within the golf swing (often described as the X factor in golf literature). However, if a golfer is unable to close this separation as contact is approached, there will be no transfer of this potential energy into functional, active kinetic energy, and high club-head speeds will not be produced. It is only when the separation is closed that true power can be achieved safely and effectively. Once contact has been achieved, these same muscles help slow the body down during the follow-through phase to keep the joints and ligaments safe. Use this exercise to help you learn how to both create and then eliminate separation between the pelvis and shoulders.

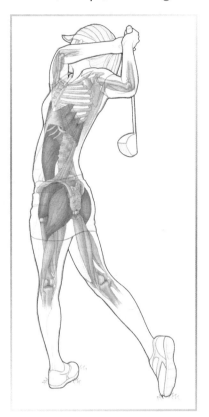

---

## VARIATION

### Trunk Rotation Throw on Stability Ball

Perform this version with a partner to incorporate a little more explosiveness into the exercise. Make sure to keep the same form with the body and hands. If the partner is on your left, release the medicine ball to him as you rotate left, and catch it from him overhead as you are rotating back to the right.

# Walking Lunge With Twist

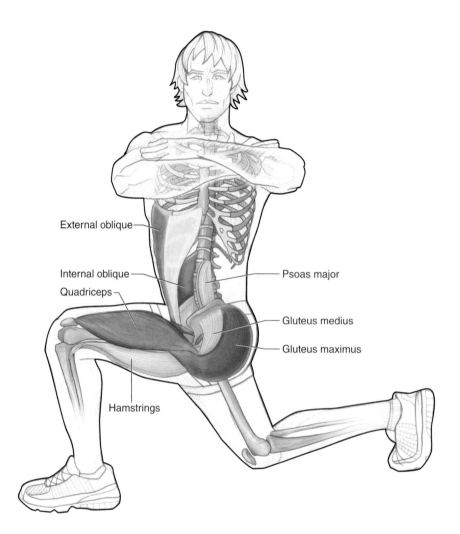

External oblique

Internal oblique

Quadriceps

Hamstrings

Psoas major

Gluteus medius

Gluteus maximus

## Execution

1. Stand with feet shoulder-width apart.
2. Step forward with your left foot, and drop your right knee down just above the ground without letting your left knee go past your toes.
3. Cross your arms over your chest, and rotate your torso to the left.
4. Rotate back to center, return to the start position, and repeat on the opposite side.

## Muscles Involved

**Primary:** Quadriceps, gluteus maximus, external oblique, internal oblique

**Secondary:** Gluteus medius, hamstrings, psoas major

## Golf Focus

Maintaining proper body angles during this exercise is just as important as it is during the golf swing. Once down into the lunge, the legs must work a little bit harder to stabilize and resist the movements caused when you rotate your torso. This same principle is needed in both the backswing and the downswing to prevent the sway and slide of the hips. For proper rotation of the torso to occur, you must also have a completely straight alignment of the spine. However, at many points in the swing, this must all be done while the hips, knees, and ankles remain relatively stable. These lunges help you gain this stability and strength in your lower body. The twist portion of the exercise will help you train your ability to rotate your torso around fixed hips. Being able to control both of these will lead to better energy transfer and more consistent ball striking.

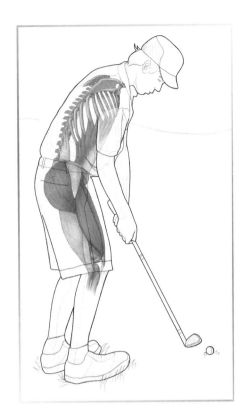

---

### VARIATION

### Walking Lunge With Twist With Golf Club

Perform the same exercise, but place a golf club between your hands and upper arms. As you turn, stay upright and keep the club parallel to the ground. This position reduces motion in the upper back and requires you to increase mobility in the lower spine and oblique musculature.

# Dolphin to Plank

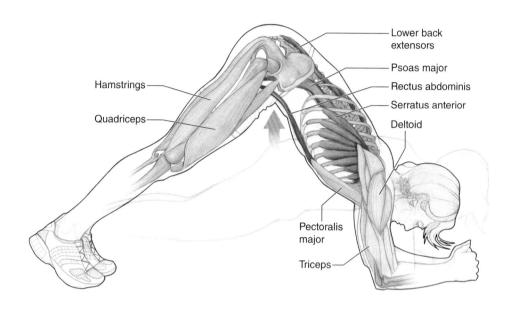

## Execution

1. Start with your forearms and toes on the ground in a plank position.
2. Push your butt up into the air while pulling your tailbone under your pelvis toward your abdomen.
3. You can straighten your knees if you like, but if your upper back rounds, it's best to keep your knees bent.
4. Hold 30 to 60 seconds. Release your knees to the floor as you exhale.
5. Return to the starting plank position and repeat for the desired number of repetitions (1 to 3).

## Muscles Involved

**Primary:** Rectus abdominis, lower back extensors, psoas major, serratus anterior

**Secondary:** Pectoralis major, triceps, hamstrings, quadriceps, deltoid

## Golf Focus

Unlike hitting balls at the driving range, on the golf course it is rare to find a perfect lie. At times the ball will be below your feet, and at other times it will be above your feet. Sometimes you will be in the rough and sometimes in the sand. Then there are those marvelous occasions when the ball is below your feet and buried somewhere in the rough. To top it off, sometimes you get into a situation where you have one of these lies and you have a long iron or rescue club in your hands. In these instances, it is important to have the flexibility to comfortably get yourself into a good setup position when addressing the ball and then have the strength and stability to maintain your positions as you attempt to progress the ball 200-plus yards onto the green. The moments when you successfully pull off these types of shots on the course are what keep you coming back and help you achieve better and better scores.

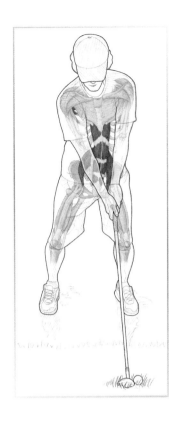

## VARIATION

## Downward Dog

If the forearm version of this exercise is easy for you to perform, try the exercise with your hands on the ground instead of your forearms, in a push-up type position. From this position, push your butt up into the air while pulling your tailbone under your pelvis toward your abdomen. You can straighten your knees if you like, but if your upper back rounds, it's best to keep your knees bent.

# High Plank Knee-Unders

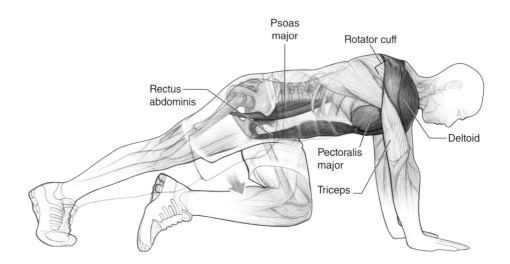

## Execution

1. Start in a push-up position with your hands under your shoulders and your elbows straight. Your body is as straight as a plank of wood.
2. Lift your left foot off the ground slowly, and bend your left knee up to your left hip.
3. Slightly push the left knee under the right thigh; pause.
4. Return to the start position. Repeat with the right leg.

## Muscles Involved

**Primary:** Deltoid, pectoralis major, rectus abdominis, psoas major
**Secondary:** Triceps, rotator cuff

## Golf Focus

When playing out of thick rough, it is important to be able to create proper separation of the pelvis and torso while possessing the strength to maintain your positions while driving the club head through the thick grass. When the body isn't able to create and maintain the separation, the end result is a loss of club-head momentum and the ball remaining in the rough. Not the most desirable result!

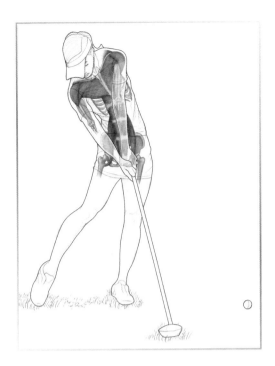

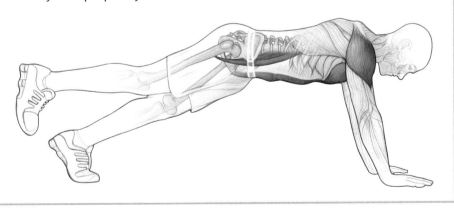

### VARIATION

## High Plank With Hip Extension

Try this exercise if the other one is still a little difficult for you. Hold the plank position while lifting one leg off the ground for 10 to 15 seconds. This will strengthen the muscles that stabilize your body and prepare you for the other exercise.

# Spider-Man Push-Up

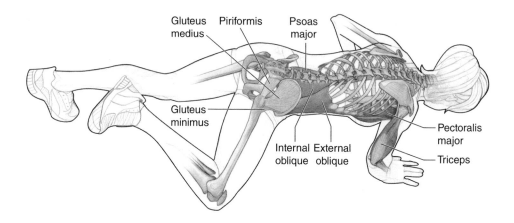

## Execution

1. Get into a push-up position.
2. As you go down into the push-up, bend your right knee up toward your right hand while trying to get your inner thigh parallel to the ground. Try to limit pelvis motion by using mostly hip motion.
3. Return to the start position and repeat with the opposite leg.

## Muscles Involved

**Primary:** Pectoralis major, triceps, external oblique, internal oblique, psoas major

**Secondary:** Gluteus medius, gluteus minimus, piriformis

## Golf Focus

Strength and mobility are needed in almost every golf shot. Some shots require more than others. Trying to hit shots that involve both an awkward stance and a high level of power can be close to impossible without proper hip and torso mobility. Many golfers lack sufficient hip motion for normal golf shots, so attempting more difficult shots can easily lead to injury without proper training. Spider-Man push-ups address this need and train upper body and torso strength while simultaneously working on hip mobility. This will allow you to still provide power to shots that lock up your feet in unnatural positions. This synergy of strength and mobility is a common theme within many parts of the golf swing and is needed not only with simple fairway shots but also those that require awkward stances.

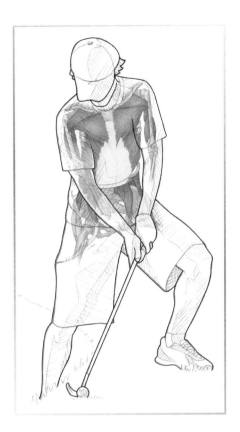

<br>

## VARIATION

### Elevated Spider-Man Push-Up

Perform the same exercise, but place your hands on a bench. This will make the push-up much easier as well as allow more room for the hip to bend and rotate. This variation is for the golfer who either lacks strength for a normal push-up or lacks enough hip mobility to clear the ground.

# V-Sit With Rotation and Single-Arm Reach

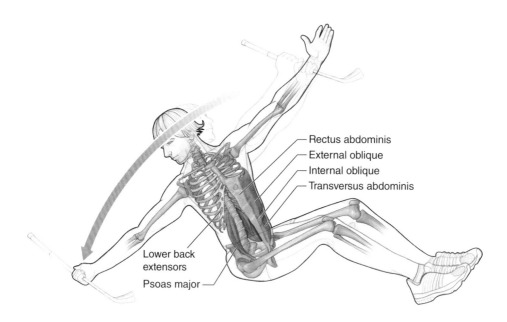

Rectus abdominis
External oblique
Internal oblique
Transversus abdominis

Lower back
extensors
Psoas major

## Execution

1. Sit with your knees bent, legs together, and heels on the ground. Your arms should be straight out in front of you, with both hands grasping a golf club.
2. Lean back slightly until you feel your abs contract. You should have a normal arch in your lower back.
3. Club in hand, reach back with the right arm, rotating your torso and head at the same time.
4. Contract the abdominals on the left side and return to the start position.
5. Repeat on the left side.

## Muscles Involved

**Primary:** Psoas major, transversus abdominis, internal oblique, external oblique

**Secondary:** Lower back extensors, rectus abdominis

## Golf Focus

Maintaining a large radius with a straight lead arm as the downswing begins requires a great deal of flexibility between the pelvic, abdominal, and shoulder regions. A limitation in any of these areas will result in a shortened radius (bent elbow) between the shoulder and hand. This results in poor sequencing and decreased power generation. A loss of radius also requires other compensations to occur throughout the body for a square club face to be achieved at impact.

# Reverse Woodchop With Medicine Ball

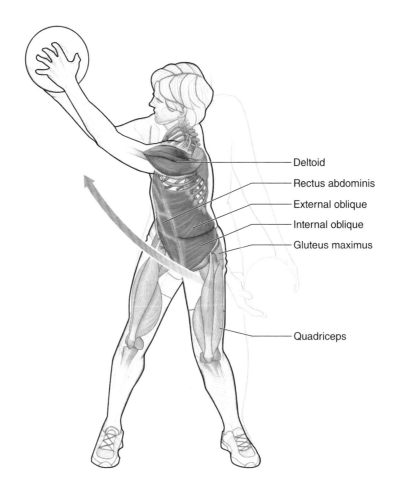

Deltoid

Rectus abdominis

External oblique

Internal oblique

Gluteus maximus

Quadriceps

## Execution

1. Stand in an athletic position with hips and knees slightly bent and feet shoulder-width apart. Hold a medicine ball in both hands, and reach with the ball just below the outside of the left knee.

2. Keeping your back straight and shoulders back, slowly stand up while rotating and reaching overhead and diagonally to your right. Your weight should be on your right leg.

3. Slowly return to the start position. Perform the desired number of repetitions. Repeat in the other direction.

## Muscles Involved

**Primary:** Rectus abdominis, internal oblique, external oblique, deltoid

**Secondary:** Quadriceps, gluteus maximus

## Golf Focus

The highly rotational aspect of the golf swing causes tremendous stresses on the body, and the fact that golf is a one-sided sport makes the potential for injury even higher. The body hates asymmetry, and when it is present, body movement patterns will change and injury risks will elevate. Reverse woodchops will help to not only ensure rotational mobility but also strengthen motions opposite to those of the golf swing, which will promote physical symmetry and reduce risk of injury. The muscles responsible for these opposite motions can also be seen as decelerating muscles in the golf swing. Deceleration is very important in golf, as it allows for stabilization and the transfer of energy all the way to the club head. So despite the fact that you swing a golf club in only one direction, you must also train the muscles that appear to do the opposite.

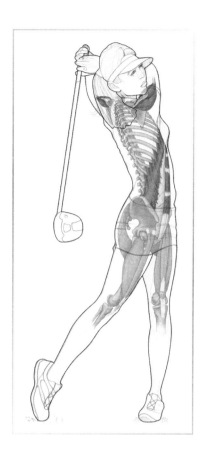

---

### VARIATION

## Reverse Woodchop With Cable Machine

You can also use a cable machine for this exercise. Attach a rope to a low pulley and follow the same motion. The use of the cable will make the dynamics slightly different, as the cable motion will be more restricted. This makes correct posture and stabilization throughout the exercise even more important.

# STABILITY FOR A CONSISTENT SWING

# CHAPTER 3

**S**tabilization is a multifaceted concept with far-reaching influences with respect to performance and safety within the golf swing. As stated in the last chapter, mobility is very important, but inability to control an enhanced range of motion can increase injury risk and cause greater inconsistency in ball striking. When considering the significance of stabilization, it is necessary to recognize that there are different layers of stability. These layers range from the segmental, or single-joint, level to the more complex multijoint and whole-body levels.

However, before we talk about the various layers of stability required by golfers, we must first create a true understanding of stability. Many people have heard the term *stability* but do not fully understand or appreciate what it is or how a lack of stability negatively affects the golf swing. We have found that the best way to illustrate the importance of stability to golfers is to provide an exaggerated visual of what consequences *instability* can have on their performance. The example we use is of Hunter Mahan hitting drives on a flat practice facility with short, perfect grass and a new pair of spikes in his shoes. You can almost feel his shoes grip into the ground as he swings through the ball. Picturing his swing, you can appreciate the force his legs generate as they push down into the ground and then transfer that energy along the chain up through his legs into his pelvis, core, and arms and finally through the club and into the ball.

This image of Hunter hitting a well-struck drive is an easy example to illustrate stability in the golf swing. Now try to imagine what Hunter's golf swing and ball flight might look like if he were hitting the ball while standing on a skateboard. The skateboard wheels provide minimal friction with the ground, which allows for greatly reduced stability. As such, there is no force to stabilize the skateboard and Hunter to the ground. When he attempts to take a backswing, the skateboard will move forward, and he will be unable to stabilize. If he is not able to push into the ground, he can't create or transfer energy from the ground up through his body into the club. If Hunter was actually able to connect with a ball while standing on a skateboard, the ball would not go very far, and he would have little to no control over which direction the ball goes.

In the body, when one part is not anchored to the adjacent body part, this area acts just like the skateboard in the previous example. This results in a loss of both energy and efficiency. Your body's muscles, tendons, and ligaments are responsible for creating stability at their respective joints. Each of these tissues has components within them that act as sensors to determine the amount of movement occurring at a specific joint. When these sensors are working optimally, they are able to sense small changes in movement at a specific joint, and the body uses this information to determine which muscles to activate in order to stabilize the movement. When the sensors are not working optimally, because of either disuse or injury, the joint will move through a greater range of motion than desired. This leads to stress on the joint and a loss of energy transfer. Proper stabilization throughout the swing allows for efficient energy transfer to occur from the ground, to the hips, to the torso, to the arms, and finally to the club head at impact (figure 3.1). Each part that lacks stability leads to a greater loss of power and consistency within the swing.

A relatively common area within the body where golfers experience instability is the hips. The muscles that connect the legs to the pelvis are often underdeveloped and act as the skateboard we just discussed. The hips slide past the target leg as the golfer moves through the ball in the downswing and the impact phase of the golf swing. This sliding prevents proper rotation at the hip joint, which also prevents the golfer from properly shifting her weight onto the target

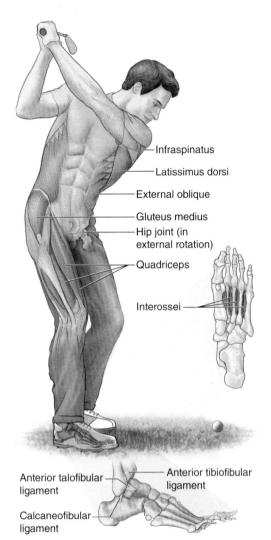

Infraspinatus
Latissimus dorsi
External oblique
Gluteus medius
Hip joint (in external rotation)
Quadriceps
Interossei

Anterior talofibular ligament
Anterior tibiofibular ligament
Calcaneofibular ligament

**Figure 3.1** Stabilization of the body, from feet through torso to arms, creates the most efficient energy transfer. Key stabilization muscles of the core and the feet.

leg (left leg in a right-handed golfer). Most golfers who have instability in the pelvis tend to slice the ball as well as place a great deal of stress on the lower back. In many cases, sliding is caused by both poor technique and weak, underdeveloped, and poorly utilized muscles of hip rotation and stabilization. When these muscles do not work correctly, the hip, pelvis, and spine cannot anchor to one another to allow for efficient and safe transfer of energy during the swing.

This is just one example of how instability within the body can negatively affect golf performance. It is necessary to develop stability at each joint on a segmental level before attaining stability throughout the body as a single functional unit. As an example, to attain stability in your shoulders, you must first create stability where the shoulder blade meets the ribs and spine and also where the shoulder blade meets the arm. If an imbalance in the muscles and ligaments is seen at either of these joints, total shoulder instability will occur. The single joints must be considered first before looking at the shoulder as a whole. The arm must be anchored to the shoulder blade, and the shoulder blade must be anchored to the ribs and spine. Once both single-joint and multijoint stability is achieved, proper muscle contraction and energy transfer can occur.

This chapter has been designed to help you, the golfer, create stability at the three areas we believe are the most important for the golf swing: the shoulder, spine, and pelvis. The pelvis allows energy created by the legs to be transmitted into the spine and core, and the shoulders allow energy within the spine and core to be transferred into the arms and finally the club. Once you have learned how to properly stabilize and isolate your shoulders, spine, and pelvis, you can find exercises that require you to integrate stabilization across these areas in full-body movements.

The exercises in this chapter span a range of difficulty. Unless stated otherwise, try to perform 8 to 15 repetitions for each exercise, depending on your fitness level and the difficulty of the exercise. Use correct form; if you need to perform fewer than 8 repetitions to maintain correct form, do so until you work up to 8. Complete 3 sets of each exercise. As you improve, increase the number of repetitions in each set. Most exercises use only body weight. For those that require resistance, use a weight that allows you to complete 3 sets of 15 repetitions before increasing the weight. As you improve, increase resistance and attempt to complete 3 sets of 8 repetitions.

# Ts

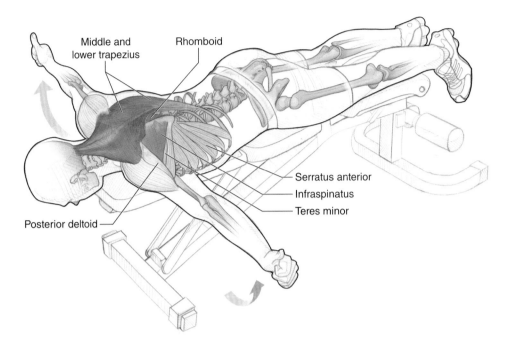

## Execution

1. Lie flat on a bench on your abdomen, with your arms hanging toward the floor. Elbows should be straight and your thumbs pointed up.
2. Slowly bring your shoulder blades together and away from your ears without moving your arms.
3. Raise your straight arms slowly to the sides so that you create a T with your body and arms. Do not shrug your shoulders.
4. Hold for 2 counts and then slowly return to the start position.

## Muscles Involved

**Primary:** Rhomboid, middle trapezius, lower trapezius, infraspinatus

**Secondary:** Teres minor, serratus anterior, posterior deltoid

## Golf Focus

During the downswing, it is important for the target-side shoulder blade to pull hard toward the spine and down and away from the ears. When this happens, the shoulder blade becomes anchored to the core and torso. This allows the left arm to pull hard and allows the golfer to transfer his weight onto the target-side leg (left leg in a right-handed golfer). When the lead shoulder blade is not pulled down and instead is shrugged up toward the ears, it makes it difficult for a golfer to transfer weight onto the lead side and instead pushes the golfer's weight onto the back leg. This decreases the power a golfer is able to generate, increases the stress on the lower back, and often results in a slice as the golfer holds onto the club through impact.

---

## VARIATION

### Ws

This variation works the same muscles but in a slightly different way since the arms are in a different position. Ws may be easier to begin with if you find that Ts are a bit challenging. Perform the W variation the same way you did the T, except bend your elbows to 90 degrees. Keep your thumbs pointed toward the ceiling.

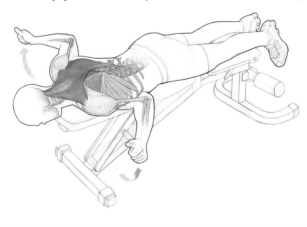

# High to Low With Shoulder Retraction

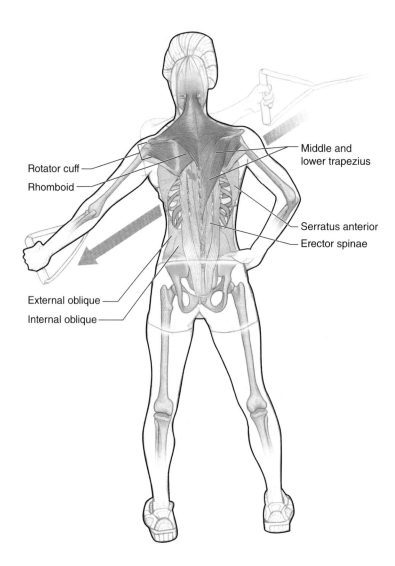

Rotator cuff

Rhomboid

Middle and
lower trapezius

Serratus anterior

Erector spinae

External oblique

Internal oblique

## Execution

1. Hold the handle of a resistance band with your left arm extended across the front of your chest. Your right hand is resting on your waist.

2. Pull your left shoulder blade in toward your spine and down and away from your ears while pulling the handle across your body in a diagonal fashion until it is outside your left hip.

3. Keep the left arm straight the whole time.

4. Return to the start position and complete the desired number of repetitions. Switch arms and perform the exercise with the right arm.

## Muscles Involved

**Primary:** Middle trapezius, lower trapezius, rhomboid, rotator cuff

**Secondary:** External oblique, internal oblique, erector spinae, serratus anterior

## Golf Focus

As every golfer knows, it is important to be able to hit down through
the golf ball to either create compression of the ball into the ground
or drive through the rough or wet
sand. If you are not able to drive
down through the ball, there will
not be a transfer of energy into the
ball, and a mis-hit will occur. As
described in the Ts and Ws exercises, it is very important for golfers
to create stability in the target-side
shoulder in order to pull themselves
onto the lead leg at impact. It is
also important for golfers to be able
to stabilize the core as they drive
hard onto the target side. This is a
great exercise to teach you how to
stabilize your core area while learning how to pull your shoulder blade
down and move your arms across
your body into the golf ball.

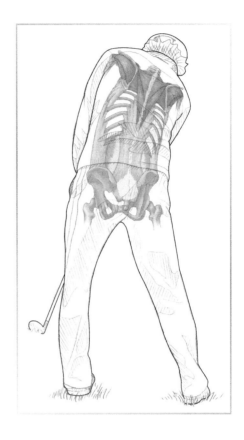

# Side-Lying External Hip Rotation

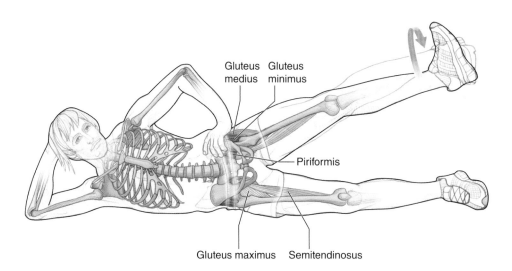

Gluteus medius   Gluteus minimus

Piriformis

Gluteus maximus    Semitendinosus

## Execution

1. Lie on your side with both legs straight. Your body should form a straight line from head to feet.
2. Keeping your leg straight, raise your top leg 12 inches into the air. This is the start position.
3. Rotate at the hip joint and turn the top leg so your toes point toward the ceiling.
4. Return to the start position and repeat the desired number of repetitions. Switch sides and repeat with the other leg.

## Muscles Involved

**Primary:** Piriformis, posterior aspect of gluteus medius, gluteus minimus

**Secondary:** Semitendinosus, gluteus maximus

## Golf Focus

During the downswing, it is important for the lead leg to create a
stable base to allow the pelvis to
rotate efficiently toward the target.
When the muscles that attach from
the hip to the pelvis are weak (as
they are with most people!), the
pelvis will have a tendency to slide
too far toward the target during the
downswing, which will prevent the
hips from rotating. The end result
is a player unable to create room
for her arms to move through. This
causes her to block or slice the ball.
This is one of the more common
causes of blocked shots and slices
on the course.

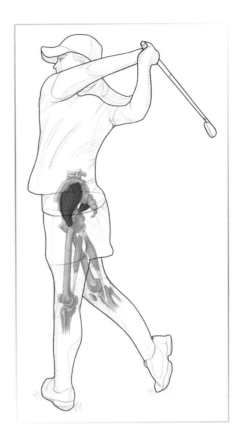

# Side Leg Lift With Inward Rotation

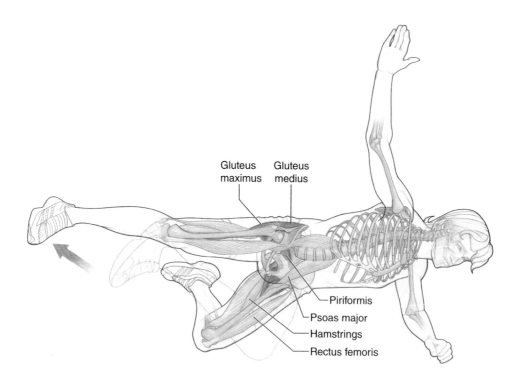

Gluteus maximus  
Gluteus medius  
Piriformis  
Psoas major  
Hamstrings  
Rectus femoris

## Execution

1. Lie on your left forearm and left knee with your body in a straight line from head to toes.
2. Raise your right arm over your head and your top leg 12 inches into the air. This is the start position.
3. Bend the hip and knee of the top leg to 90 degrees. The top knee should be at the level of your bottom hip.
4. Straighten your top leg back to the start position by squeezing the muscles of your buttocks.
5. Complete the desired number of repetitions. Switch sides and repeat with the other leg.

## Muscles Involved

**Primary:** Gluteus maximus, gluteus medius, piriformis

**Secondary:** Hamstrings, psoas major, rectus femoris

## Golf Focus

As mentioned in the previous exercise, a weakness in the muscles
connecting the hip to the pelvis
will result in the pelvis sliding
toward the target and a reduced
ability to rotate the pelvis toward
the target at impact. When these
muscles are strong and working
properly, the golfer is able to post
hard on the lead leg in the downswing and at impact, which allows
him to efficiently transfer energy
generated in the legs through the
core and into the arms, making it
easier to hit more powerful and
accurate shots. This movement is
made easier when there is proper
mobility within the hip joint itself.
For this reason it is important to go
through the exercises in the mobility section of this book.

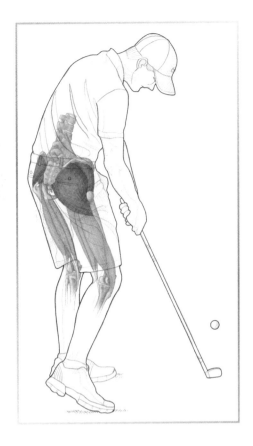

# Supine Abdominal Toes and Heels

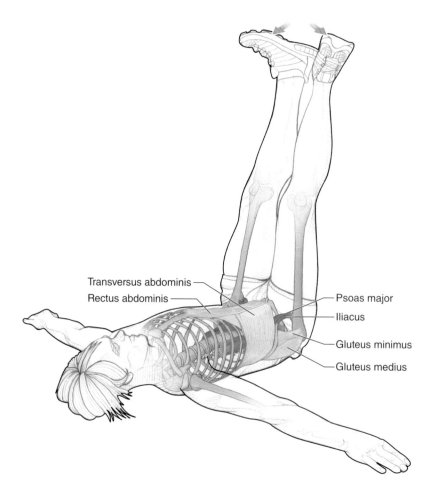

Transversus abdominis
Rectus abdominis
Psoas major
Iliacus
Gluteus minimus
Gluteus medius

## Execution

1. Lie on your back with legs raised to between 60 and 90 degrees (straight at the knee).
2. With your heels touching (they should remain touching throughout the exercise), slowly rotate through the hips to separate your toes from each other.
3. Rotate through the hips back to the start position.
4. Repeat for the desired number of repetitions.

## Muscles Involved

**Primary:** Psoas major, iliacus, piriformis

**Secondary:** Rectus abdominis, transversus abdominis, gluteus medius, gluteus minimus

## Golf Focus

One of the more common swing faults associated with amateur golfers is early extension and a loss of spinal posture before contact with the ball. This flaw becomes more apparent when long clubs are used because the greater length of the club's shaft increases the forces that must be absorbed by the body. Many golfers say they do not have a problem with maintaining their posture and angles with the shorter clubs but are not able to do so with the longer irons, woods, and driver. Strengthening the psoas major is very important for any golfer who struggles with maintaining posture through the downswing and impact. The psoas major (hip flexor) attaches from your spine to your leg, and when this muscle is weak, it is not able to withstand the high forces of the longer clubs and is unable to hold the shortened length. The hip flexor lengthens under high loads, and this is seen as a loss of spinal posture before impact.

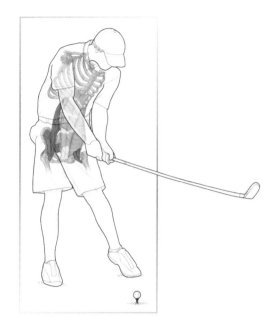

## VARIATION

### Supine Abdominal Reverse Heels and Toes

Perform this variation in the same position, except this time keep your toes touching and rotate your heels. This will challenge the same muscles, but they will be stressed differently because of the opposite rotation of the feet and hips.

# Prone Back Extension

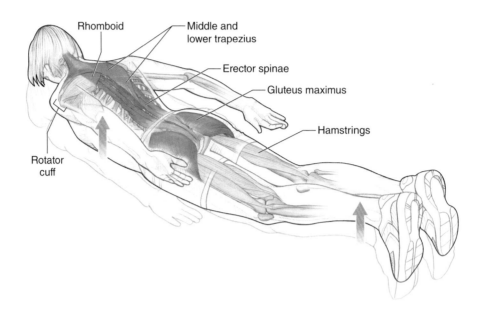

Rhomboid

Middle and lower trapezius

Erector spinae

Gluteus maximus

Hamstrings

Rotator cuff

## Execution

1. Lie facedown with your legs together, arms at your sides with palms up.
2. Lift your upper body, arms, and legs slightly off the ground by squeezing the muscles between your shoulder blades and buttocks.
3. Maintain good neck alignment by looking down at the floor for the duration of the exercise.
4. Hold for 2 to 5 slow breaths.
5. Return to the start position and repeat.

## Muscles Involved

**Primary:** Rhomboid, middle trapezius, lower trapezius, gluteus maximus, erector spinae

**Secondary:** Hamstrings, rotator cuff

## Golf Focus

As you explode from your backswing, your body must be able to properly stabilize at the shoulder complex, pelvis, and spine while simultaneously progressing through a variety of different movements. To properly perform these actions in your golf swing, it is important that you train your body as one functional unit in your fitness programs. This is a great exercise to perform as a means of developing strength and stability along the entire back half of your body. Concentrate on lengthening and elongating your whole body from the top of your head to the tips of your toes. It is also important that you focus on your breathing, making sure that your rib cage is expanding as you inhale. Perform this exercise cautiously, and consult your doctor if you experience any back pain.

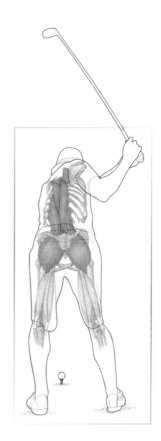

---

### VARIATION

## Prone T Back Extension

Perform the same exercise, except this time keep your arms straight out in the form of a T, with your thumbs toward the ceiling. This will increase the challenge to your middle and lower traps. Do not let your shoulders lift toward your ears, which will allow your upper trapezius to dominate.

# Full Side Plank

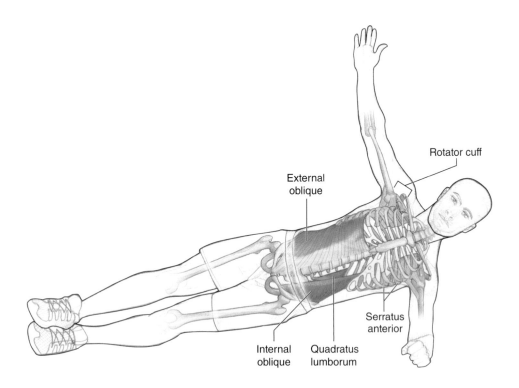

## Execution

1. Lie on your left side with your right leg on top of your left. Rest on your left forearm with your elbow directly under your shoulder.
2. Push yourself up onto your left forearm and left foot so that your feet, knees, hips, and shoulders are all in one straight line.
3. Maintain this position without dropping your hips or torso, rolling your pelvis backward, or bending at the waist.
4. Hold until form breaks, and then perform on the opposite side.
5. Repeat 3 to 5 times on each side.

## Muscles Involved

**Primary:** External oblique, internal oblique, quadratus lumborum

**Secondary:** Serratus anterior, rotator cuff

## Golf Focus

Golf would be much easier if every swing were from the same position with no fluctuations in ground slope, length of grass, or hardness of sand and no obstructions on the course. Since this is not the case, you must be prepared to execute your swing in many different situations. This exercise not only gives you the strength needed for standard shots but also prepares you for those that require an extra amount of stability. A good, clean release of the ball can be tricky from deep rough. Without enough strength to stabilize the pelvis and lower back, it can be next to impossible. The full side plank will help you achieve this strength so that you can withstand the pressure of high-velocity swings that will encounter resistance such as deep rough.

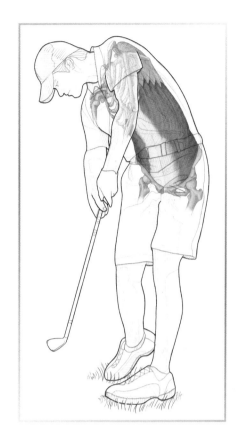

## VARIATION

### Side Plank With Hip Drop

Once you can perform the full side plank for long durations without losing form, progress to this variation. Make the muscles work even harder by dropping the hips a couple of inches (several centimeters), holding for 2 counts, then pressing back to the start. Make sure to control all movement from the hip and pelvis area, not the shoulder.

# Single-Leg Horizontal Chop

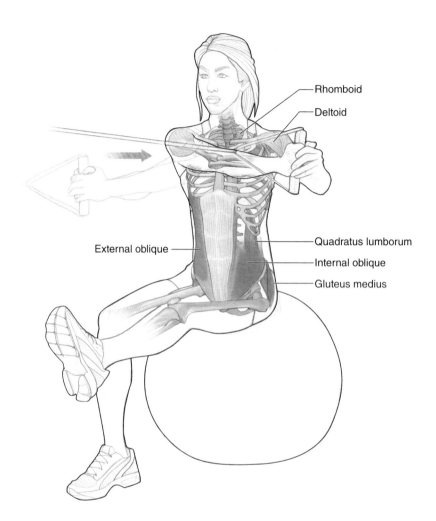

Rhomboid

Deltoid

Quadratus lumborum

External oblique

Internal oblique

Gluteus medius

## Execution

1. Sit on a stability ball with your left leg off the ground, your right leg on the floor, and your right knee and hip bent 90 degrees.
2. Attach resistance tubing to a stable object directly to your right.
3. Hold the tubing handle in both hands, with elbows locked and arms straight out in front of you. Tubing should be at a 90-degree angle to your arms.
4. Keep your head and knees pointing forward while you rotate your torso fully to the left.
5. Perform the desired number of repetitions. Repeat on the opposite side.

## Muscles Involved

**Primary:** Gluteus medius, external oblique, internal oblique, quadratus lumborum

**Secondary:** Deltoid, rhomboid

## Golf Focus

The golf swing presents the body with many challenges because of the large ranges of motion involved and the highly rotational aspect of the sport. Many people do not have difficulty balancing on two feet, but add a high-speed golf swing to the mix, and instability can be seen in many parts of the body. This exercise begins to train the stability of your hips while incorporating a resisted rotational component. Every swing you take on the golf course requires you to stabilize your hips while you rotate your torso around them. Without this key ability, many swing faults will develop, and consistent ball striking will never occur. Keep your feet, knees, and hips all in one line during the exercise without moving from side to side. This will help prevent swaying and sliding in your golf swing and give you a solid base from which to swing.

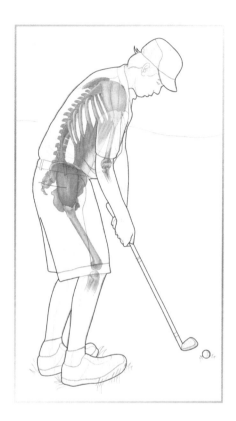

## VARIATION

### Single-Leg Horizontal Chop With Cable

This exercise can also be performed with an adjustable cable machine and a pulley handle. Place the cable at shoulder height so that it is at a 90-degree angle to your body at the start position. Perform the same motion.

# T Push-Up

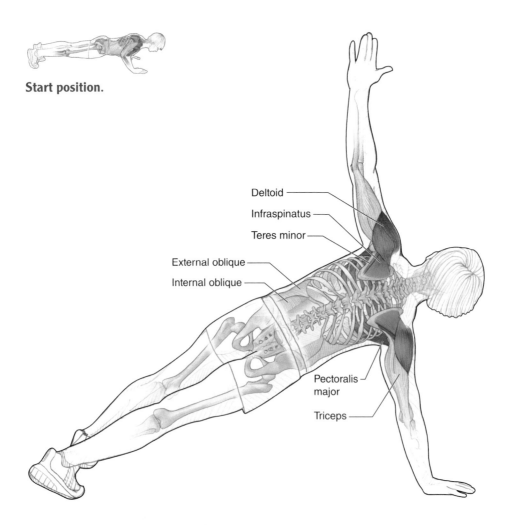

**Start position.**

Deltoid
Infraspinatus
Teres minor
External oblique
Internal oblique
Pectoralis major
Triceps

## Execution

1. Begin in a push-up position.
2. Do a normal push-up, but on the way up balance on your right hand, lift up your left hand, and rotate your torso to the left.
3. Turn until your chest is facing directly to the left and your left hand is pointing straight to the ceiling.
4. Return slowly to the starting push-up position and repeat on the opposite side.

## Muscles Involved

**Primary:** Infraspinatus, teres minor, deltoid, pectoralis major

**Secondary:** Triceps, external oblique, internal oblique

## Golf Focus

To prevent releasing the club early in the downswing, you have to maintain proper arm and shoulder angles. The strength and stability required to do this increases as the length of the club increases. Therefore, when you are required to utilize one of your fairway woods for a second shot, this shoulder stability becomes crucial for avoiding poor swing technique. T push-ups not only strengthen the stabilizing muscles of the shoulder but also help you gain greater control over these muscles. To do this exercise correctly, you must generate most of the movement from your planted shoulder. Pivoting the body around the shoulder places great demand on these muscles. This will enable you to control your swing at a much higher level.

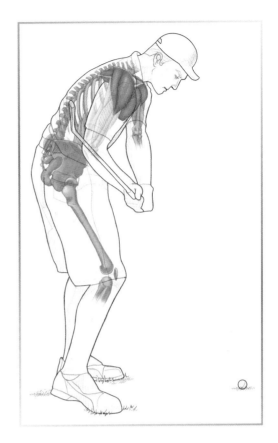

## VARIATION

### T Push-Up With Dumbbells

Perform the same exercise except with the use of 5 to 10 pound (2.5 to 5 kg) dumbbells. This will work the same muscles but presents a much greater challenge to the stabilizing muscles. Progress to the variation only when ready because this exercise also challenges the wrist stabilizers.

# Push-Up With Medicine Ball

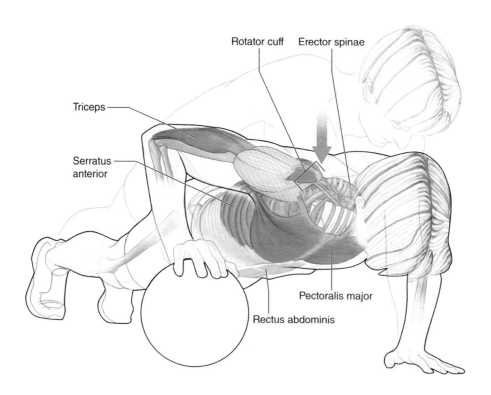

## Execution

1. Get into a push-up position, but place a medium-size medicine ball under your right hand.
2. Slowly go down into the lower position of the push-up without losing your straight, neutral spine.
3. Return to the start position.
4. Perform the desired number of repetitions. Place the medicine ball under the opposite hand and repeat.

## Muscles Involved

**Primary:** Pectoralis major, triceps, serratus anterior, rotator cuff

**Secondary:** Rectus abdominis, erector spinae

## Golf Focus

Transferring energy from the ground to the club requires many body parts to work in conjunction. Once the energy reaches your upper torso, the shoulders become important in transferring this energy to the club. Using a medicine ball to perform push-ups places a demand on your muscles that trains the fine movements and responsiveness of your shoulders. As you near impact, the shoulders must be stable to effectively transfer all energy to the hands and club without losing any speed or power. Placing one of your hands on a medicine ball also trains slightly different areas of the muscles since your hands are on different levels. This ensures more muscle fiber activation as well as increased demand due to stabilization requirements.

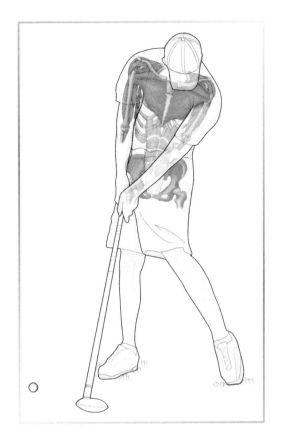

## Push-Up on Stability Ball

This variation greatly increases the demand on your body because the stability ball creates much more instability. You will be working the same muscles, however. Since both hands are in an unstable environment, much of the muscle contraction will be used to maintain balance before movement can even occur.

# Rotating Side Plank

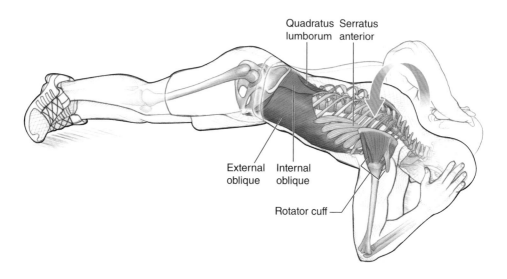

Quadratus lumborum

Serratus anterior

External oblique

Internal oblique

Rotator cuff

## Execution

1. Get into full side plank position (see page 64) on your left forearm, and place your right hand behind your head.
2. Slowly turn your torso, hips, and right elbow toward the floor, moving your torso and hips as one unit.
3. Generate the movement with your obliques and left shoulder. Do not just move your elbow.
4. Slowly return to the start position.
5. Perform the desired number of repetitions. Repeat on the opposite side.

## Muscles Involved

**Primary:** External oblique, internal oblique, quadratus lumborum, rotator cuff

**Secondary:** Serratus anterior

## Golf Focus

On long holes you will have to take a powerful second shot with a long club in order to get yourself close to the green. This requires increased precision with your movements as well as an increased ability to generate power. Rotating side planks not only train the muscles that assist with pelvis and torso stability but also strengthen your shoulders. This will improve your ability to create club lag to generate increased club-head speed. As club length and swing speed increase, more strength is needed to maintain proper technique. When performing this exercise, concentrate on using your obliques and shoulder muscles to complete the movement. This precision in movement during the exercise will train your muscles for a good carryover into your swing.

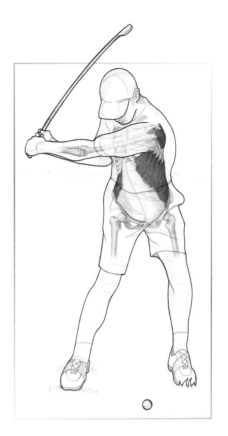

# Adductor Plank

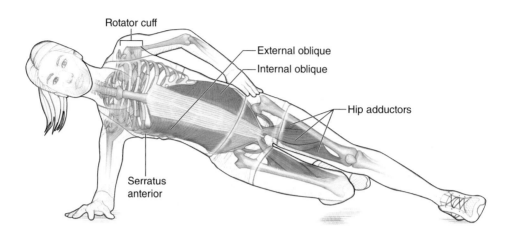

## Execution

1. Lie on your right side with your left leg straight and right leg bent 90 degrees behind you.
2. Push yourself up onto your right forearm and left foot so that your foot, knees, hips, and shoulders are all in one straight line. Keep your right leg lifted off the ground.
3. Maintain this position for as long as you can without dropping your hips or torso, rolling your pelvis backward, or bending at the waist.
4. Perform 3 to 5 repetitions. Repeat on the opposite side.

## Muscles Involved

**Primary:** Hip adductors, internal oblique, external oblique

**Secondary:** Serratus anterior, rotator cuff

## Golf Focus

The initial part of the downswing is very important in determining whether the club head will return to a proper position for impact. Allowing your arms or torso to initiate this movement can lead to many different swing faults. Golfers do this either because they have poor technique or because they have poor strength and control in the lower body muscles. To initiate the downswing, the leg muscles should engage and begin the press toward the lead leg. This initial press puts the lower body in a perfect position to continue with hip, pelvis, and trunk rotation so that proper downswing sequencing can occur. The adductor plank trains the muscles in the legs and trunk that both create this press and provide a stable environment from which to rotate.

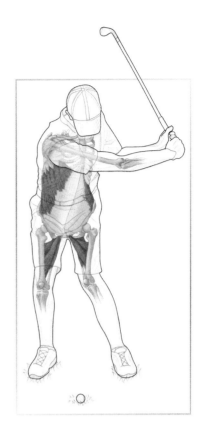

## VARIATION

### Standing Scissors

Stand with feet shoulder-width apart and to the right of a low-pulley cable machine. Use an ankle attachment on your left ankle. Standing straight on your right leg, slowly bring your left leg in front of your right leg as much as possible. Perform the desired number of repetitions and repeat with the other leg.

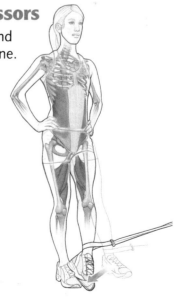

# Prone Scissor Twist

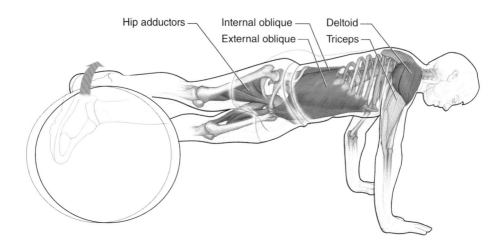

Hip adductors — | Internal oblique — | Deltoid —
External oblique — | Triceps —

## Execution

1. Get in a push-up position with a stability ball between your legs and your legs in the middle of the ball.
2. Keeping your core engaged and your spine neutral, slowly rotate the ball to your left as far as you can without allowing your back to arch.
3. Slowly return to the start position and repeat on the opposite side.

## Muscles Involved

**Primary:** External oblique, internal oblique, hip adductors, deltoid

**Secondary:** Triceps, quadratus lumborum

## Golf Focus

In an attempt to generate high swing speeds, many players try to overpower the swing with large muscles. This almost inevitably causes poor ball striking and shorter distances. Accuracy and distance are gained by utilizing the correct muscles, at the correct time, and in the correct order. In situations where you need a long club off the fairway, it is crucial that you do not allow the upper body to dominate the swing. The legs must first firmly stabilize and generate power from the ground. Then the pelvis and torso must disassociate from one another to create and transfer even more power. This step is often missed, as golfers try to kill the ball with their upper body strength. This exercise will help strengthen and reinforce the muscles that not only initiate some of these powerful movements but also help stabilize so that energy can be passed to the upper body at the correct time.

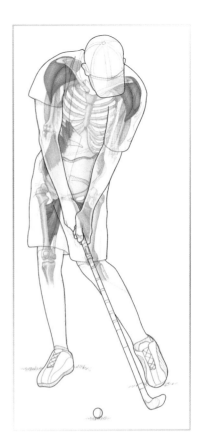

## VARIATION

### Supine Oblique Twist

The prone scissor twist is a difficult exercise to perform correctly. If you struggle with the prone scissor twist, use this variation to train the same muscles. To perform this variation, lie with your upper back against the floor. Push the backs of your hands against the ground to help keep your back stable. Use your obliques to generate and control the movement. Go only as far as you can without lifting too much of your torso off the ground.

# BALANCE AND BODY AWARENESS FOR A SOLID BASE

The number of golfers who do not perform any type of fitness program is surprising. If they do work out, it usually consists of a minimal number of exercises that are extremely nonspecific to the sport they are playing. Very few golfers incorporate balance in their routines or have even considered implementing a balance focus in their programs. However, when we analyze golfers, we often discover that just balancing on one foot can be challenging for them. How then can these golfers expect to have efficient balance during a powerful rotational movement such as the golf swing?

Every golfer, amateur or professional, knows that every golf shot is different. The distance to the target, wind speed and direction, lie of the ball, type of grass or sand, and speed of the greens are all variables outside the golfer's control. One of the greatest variables within the game of golf is the surface the golfer must stand on while addressing the ball. The ball may lie either below or above the golfer's feet, the golfer may have one foot higher than the other, the ground may be slick, or the golfer may have to stand at an awkward distance from the ball at address. Each of these variables requires the body to adjust. These adjustments must occur at rapid speeds and in a finely tuned manner. The smallest flaw in mechanics may result in an outcome that differs greatly from the golfer's initial objective. By creating more efficiency in your body's balance and training your body to adapt quickly to these environmental discrepancies, your golf shots will become more consistent, and you will be able to successfully complete more difficult shots.

Balance is a layman's term for a number of processes that occur within your body to maintain your center of gravity over a base of support. The less work you have to do to maintain this position, the better your balance is. Your ability to stay in balance is dependent on your body's ability to decipher sensory information and relay it quickly and effectively to the muscles and joints. Although this sounds very complicated, it is something you do on a daily basis without ever having to think about it. The most obvious example is of a person walking. When we walk, we don't think about what muscles should contract or in what sequence they should contract. It just sort of happens. We are able to walk without thinking about it because our bodies have learned how to do it subconsciously. Can you imagine how difficult it would be to walk if you had to think about every movement of the body and every muscle that needed to work properly? Yet many golfers try to do just that with their golf swings. The more you get into your own head and try to control every aspect of the swing, the worse your swing becomes. It is impossible to analyze and react in a movement that takes less than a few seconds. For this reason, the more balancing you can do within the subconscious, the better.

Body awareness, otherwise known as proprioception, is your ability to sense where your body is in space at any given time. This is extremely important because of the various weight shifts, rotational forces, and energy transfers found in the golf swing. A very important skill to have is being able to correctly match up "real and feel." This means that your perceptions about where your body and club are during the swing equal the reality of their actual positions. This makes lessons much more efficient and learning new skills much easier. Improved proprioception will not only increase the control you have over your body but also allow you to have better awareness of where the club is throughout the swing. Without this ability, it is very difficult to determine whether you are practicing the correct swing pattern or why a certain shot may have been mis-hit.

The golf swing happens very quickly, so these processes must occur within your body much quicker and more efficiently than in the average person. Balance and proprioception must be working at a high level in order to develop a repeatable, fluid, and functional golf swing (figure 4.1). During the swing, as weight is transferred onto the lead leg at the onset of the downswing, the pressure sensors in your feet detect changes in weight. This begins to send information to the muscles required to produce the stability and movement that ultimately result in balance. If any of this information is delayed or incorrect, the body is not able to recruit the proper muscles in the proper sequence. When this happens, the golfer has to depend on his hands to make up for poor body control during the golf swing. The end result is very inconsistent ball striking. This breakdown in communication

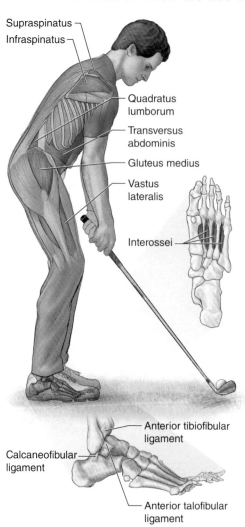

Supraspinatus
Infraspinatus
Quadratus lumborum
Transversus abdominis
Gluteus medius
Vastus lateralis
Interossei
Anterior tibiofibular ligament
Calcaneofibular ligament
Anterior talofibular ligament

Figure 4.1    Balance is the process by which the golfer maintains his center of gravity over his base of support. Key muscles for balancing in the core and feet.

will not only limit your shot-making potential but may also result in the muscles and joints being placed in positions where injury risk is elevated. In fact, decreased performance and chronic, unresolved pain are often the consequences of these dysfunctions in balance and proprioception.

Most of the exercises in this chapter incorporate movements or static positions on one foot. This is the best way to challenge your body's balance and proprioception systems. As the chapter progresses, the exercises become more difficult because you are asking your body to incorporate more movement and more power generation while still maintaining a solid base of support. This is exactly what is required in your golf swing. When you first begin these exercises, you may notice that it takes a lot of energy to remain balanced. As you improve, you will find that some of them become fairly easy. In fact, improvement in balance can often be noticed within the first few days of introducing specific exercises into your fitness program. *Significant* improvements can often take place in as little as a few weeks. On the other hand, changes in muscle strength, speed, and flexibility can take much longer to notice. However, improving your balance and body awareness can greatly enhance the effectiveness of training these other aspects.

Unless otherwise indicated, perform 8 to 15 repetitions of each exercise in this chapter. For balance and proprioception exercises, you will find that often the main difficulty is in maintaining your center of gravity. For these exercises, attempt to complete 15 repetitions. However, other exercises challenge strength as well as balance. For these exercises, 8 repetitions is sufficient. Perform 3 sets of each exercise. If weight is required, use a weight that allows you to complete 3 sets of 15 repetitions. Once you master the exercise, increase the weight and complete 3 sets of only 8 repetitions with the heavier weight.

# One-Leg Roll-Out

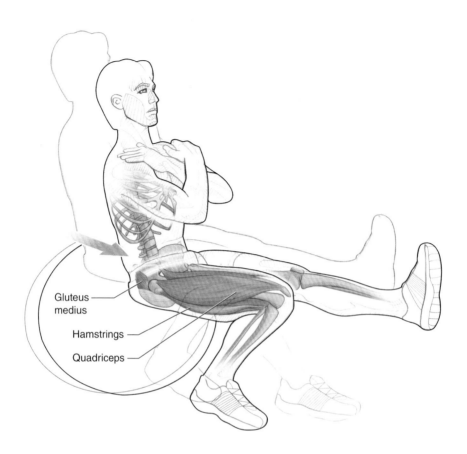

Gluteus medius

Hamstrings

Quadriceps

## Execution

1. Sit on a stability ball with your left leg parallel to the ground and your right foot on the ground out in front of you.
2. Keeping your right foot, knee, and hip in line with each other, roll forward on the ball with your right foot.
3. Roll back to the start position. Complete the desired number of repetitions and repeat with the opposite leg.

## Muscles Involved

**Primary:** Gluteus medius, hamstrings, quadriceps

**Secondary:** Hip adductors

## Golf Focus

One thing that is very difficult for many golfers is being able to match up real and feel. This means that what they feel within their swing, as far as body and club positions, actually matches what really is happening in the swing. One-leg roll-outs are a great starting point to try to achieve this body awareness in your lower body. The challenge of this exercise is not just in training the muscles of the legs but also in getting your body to better understand exactly where it is while moving. Improving this second factor will help your muscles control fine movements much better and have a much quicker reaction time. Both of these are needed to get your body to the point where you can maintain proper body position during a high-speed golf swing.

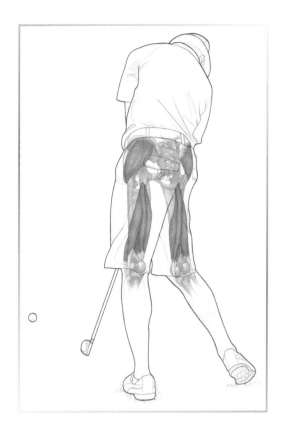

### VARIATION

## One-Leg Roll-Out With Eyes Closed

Performing this same exercise with your eyes closed will present an even greater challenge. Your eyes are typically your body's most powerful source of balance information. Without the use of sight, your feet and muscles are required to work much more aggressively to maintain balance.

# One-Leg Airplane

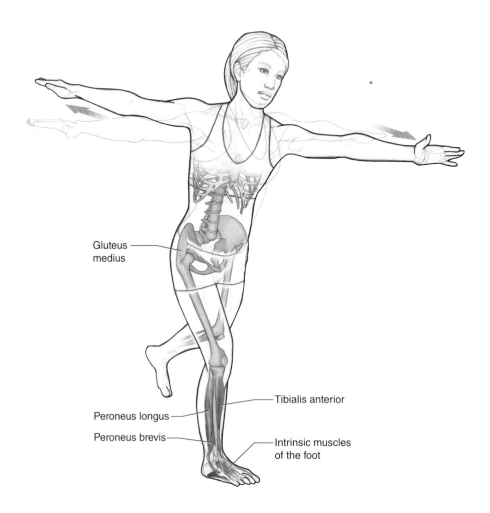

Gluteus medius

Tibialis anterior

Peroneus longus

Peroneus brevis

Intrinsic muscles of the foot

## Execution

1. Stand on your right leg with your left leg off the ground and behind you.
2. Move your arms into a T, and bend at the waist as if addressing a golf ball.
3. Keeping your right foot, knee, and hip in line with each other, rotate your torso first to the left, and then to the right.
4. Make sure to keep your arms in a T and turn with your torso.
5. Perform the desired number of repetitions and repeat on the opposite leg.

## Muscles Involved

**Primary:** Intrinsic muscles of the foot, tibialis anterior, peroneus longus, peroneus brevis

**Secondary:** Tibialis posterior, gluteus medius

## Golf Focus

Two of the major reasons that many golfers cannot make consistent flush contact with the ball are hip sway and slide. If you are unable to rotate around your hips, then the tendency is to sway (move away from the target during the backswing) or slide (move toward the target during the downswing). One thing that can limit you from achieving proper hip rotation during the swing is poor balance. This makes it very difficult to keep the club on path during your swing and therefore return the club face to the proper impact position. It also robs you of potential power that can be transferred to the club before impact. The one-leg airplane

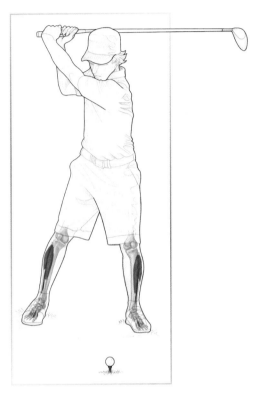

is another great exercise to train mobility and balance simultaneously. This will get you used to rotating only around your hips while keeping your foot firmly planted to the ground.

---

### VARIATION

### One-Leg Golf Swing

Incorporate this exercise directly into your golf game by performing one-leg swings. The same muscles will be worked, but trying to swing a club will be much more of a challenge. Swing at a very slow speed, and concentrate on maintaining good posture and balance throughout.

# Modified Hand-to-Toe Pose

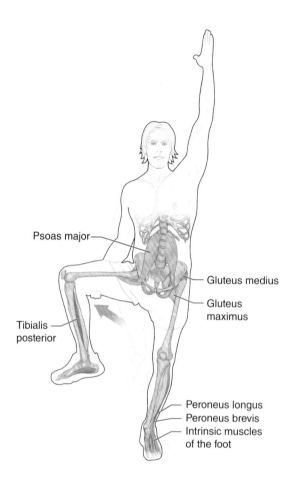

Psoas major

Gluteus medius

Gluteus maximus

Tibialis posterior

Peroneus longus
Peroneus brevis
Intrinsic muscles of the foot

## Execution

1. Stand with your legs together and your left hand reaching skyward.
2. Raise your right knee, and place your right hand underneath the outside of your thigh.
3. Stand tall, and pull your knee to hip height for 3 to 5 breaths.
4. Move your leg to the side, and hold it there for 3 to 5 breaths.
5. Repeat on the left.

## Muscles Involved

**Primary:** Intrinsic muscles of the foot, peroneus longus, peroneus brevis, tibialis posterior

**Secondary:** Gluteus medius, gluteus maximus, psoas major

## Golf Focus

Golfers at all levels can appreciate the grace and efficiency of a well-balanced swing that ends as easily and comfortably as when the golfer was in the setup. This is an easier version of the hand-to-toe yoga pose (hand holding the toes with the raised leg extended straight). The modified hand-to-toe pose develops balance, strengthens muscles of the supporting leg, and stretches the buttocks and inner thigh of the raised leg. It is a great beginner exercise to help all golfers gain a basic understanding of their ability to maintain equilibrium in a static form. When this exercise becomes easy, you can try the modification and move on to the more difficult exercises found throughout this chapter.

## VARIATION

### Hand-to-Toe Pose

The hand-to-toe pose is a more difficult exercise for two main reasons. First, it requires more flexibility through the calf, hamstrings, hip, and pelvis of the unsupported leg. Second, it requires better stabilization of the supporting leg because you have moved a greater percentage of your body's mass away from your base. In this exercise, you grab the toes of the unsupported leg and attempt to straighten the knee as you move the leg to your side. When this becomes easy, you can attempt either of the two versions with your eyes closed.

# Single-Leg Catch

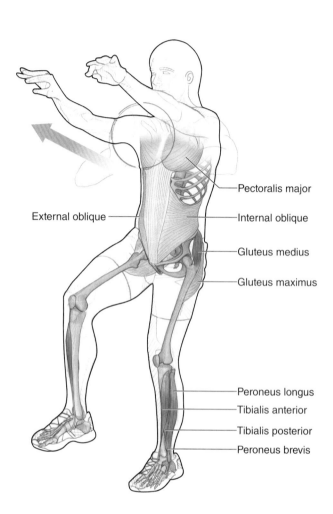

Pectoralis major

External oblique

Internal oblique

Gluteus medius

Gluteus maximus

Peroneus longus

Tibialis anterior

Tibialis posterior

Peroneus brevis

## Execution

1. Stand on your left leg with your toes pointing forward. Your right knee should be bent, with your right foot off the ground.
2. Hold a medicine ball with two hands in front of your chest.
3. While keeping your posture upright, throw a chest pass to a partner.
4. Catch the return pass with two hands while maintaining an athletic posture, left hip and knee slightly bent.
5. Perform the desired number of repetitions and repeat with the opposite leg.

## Muscles Involved

**Primary:** Tibialis anterior, tibialis posterior, peroneus longus, peroneus brevis, gluteus medius

**Secondary:** External oblique, internal oblique, gluteus maximus, pectoralis major

## Golf Focus

Maintaining balance during easy partial swings can be fairly simple. However, when you need to take full swings and apply massive speeds to achieve your shot, it becomes much more difficult. This exercise will help your legs learn how to balance efficiently while a force is being generated in your upper body. As this exercise gets easier, you can challenge this combination in a couple of ways. If you are using a partner, have the person stand farther away from you and throw the medicine ball with a much higher speed. Your partner can also throw the ball to you at different places each time instead of always throwing it to your chest (e.g., above you and to the sides so that you have to reach to make each catch). This will really teach your body how to balance effectively. As you increase the difficulty of the exercise, you will be better able to make golf shots that require both power and balance.

---

### VARIATION

### Single-Leg Catch Against Wall

If you are working out alone, get a medicine ball that bounces and throw it against a wall. The farther you are away from the wall, the harder you will have to throw the ball to make it return.

# Stork Turn

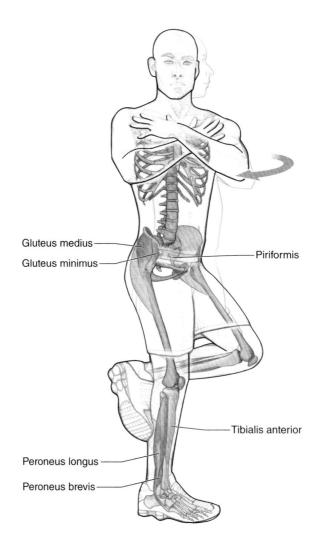

Gluteus medius
Gluteus minimus
Piriformis
Tibialis anterior
Peroneus longus
Peroneus brevis

## Execution

1. Stand on your right leg with a slightly bent knee, and lock your left foot behind your right knee.
2. Get into golf address position, and cross your arms over your chest.
3. Trying to keep your upper body in line with your pelvis, rotate your pelvis from side to side.
4. Repeat on the left leg.

## Muscles Involved

**Primary:** Peroneus longus, peroneus brevis, gluteus medius, gluteus minimus

**Secondary:** Tibialis anterior, tibialis posterior, piriformis

## Golf Focus

Being able to separate the lower body from the upper body is very important in golf. However, you must also be able to maintain great balance when trying to create maximum separation. When you begin to move your pelvis more freely and with more control, you will need greater balance. Stork turns will continue your development of pelvis movement and pelvis and torso separation and will challenge your balance at the same time. This will make you more equipped to create a full backswing with proper separation while still keeping a solid base beneath you. This is essential in order to set yourself up for a down-swing that is on path and full of potential power.

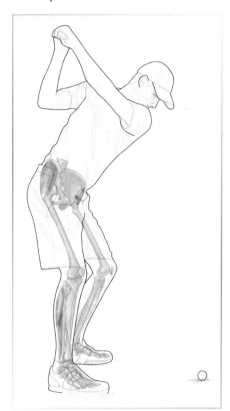

---

### VARIATION

### Stork Turn With Medicine Ball

Holding a medicine ball in front of you will make the same muscles work harder and will also challenge your deltoids, external obliques, and internal obliques. This version really forces you to simultaneously strengthen the muscles that stabilize the legs and torso and the muscles that rotate the pelvis and hips.

# Stork to Bow

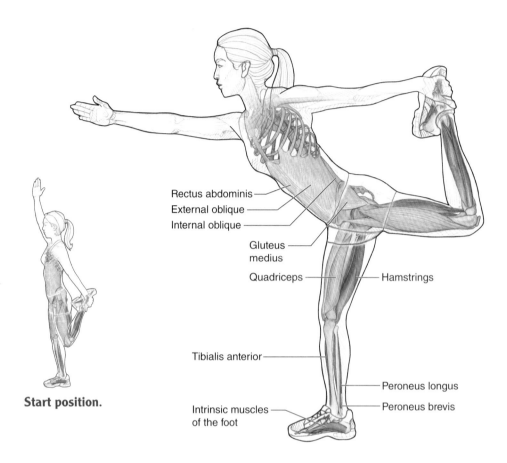

Start position.

Rectus abdominis
External oblique
Internal oblique
Gluteus medius
Quadriceps
Hamstrings
Tibialis anterior
Peroneus longus
Peroneus brevis
Intrinsic muscles of the foot

## Execution

1. Stand with your legs together.
2. Bend your left knee and hold your left ankle with your left hand.
3. Raise your right arm toward the ceiling. This is the stork position.
4. Bend forward until your torso is nearly parallel to the floor. This is the bow position.
5. Hold for 3 to 5 breaths in each position.
6. Repeat 3 to 5 times, then change legs.

## Muscles Involved

**Primary:** Peroneus longus, peroneus brevis, intrinsic muscles of the foot, tibialis anterior, hamstrings

**Secondary:** Quadriceps, gluteus medius, rectus abdominis, external oblique, internal oblique

## Golf Focus

Golf is a sport that frustrates us with its challenges and bounces, yet it rewards us when we make an amazing recovery to save par to overcome these same challenges and bounces. A frustrating moment for any golfer is discovering that the ball you were sure had stayed in the fairway had actually rolled into the fairway bunker, leaving you with a difficult shot. The ball lies 1.5 feet (.5 m) below your feet, requiring you to have great balance and stability. The stork to bow exercise helps create better balance, flexibility, and stability and will help make these difficult golf shots a little bit easier.

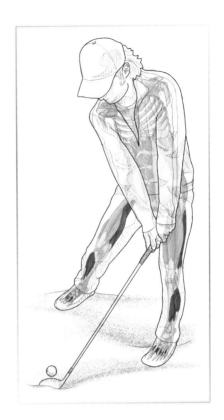

### Stork to Bow With Eyes Closed

To make this exercise even more challenging, close your eyes while moving between the stork and bow positions (just make sure there aren't any sharp objects lying around for you to bump into!). By closing your eyes, you put more emphasis on the muscles and ligaments in your feet to provide the information your body needs for even better balance and stability.

# Straight-Leg Raise on Stability Ball

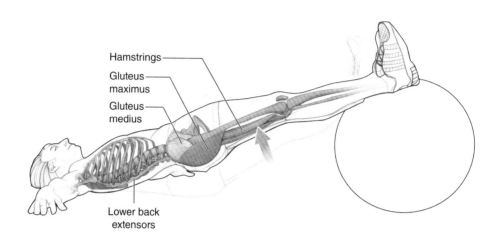

Hamstrings
Gluteus maximus
Gluteus medius
Lower back extensors

## Execution

1. Lie down with your legs straight and your heels on top of a stability ball.
2. Press down on the ball with your heels as you squeeze your gluteus muscles and lift your hips.
3. Slowly lower down to the start position.
4. Do the desired number of repetitions.

## Muscles Involved

**Primary:** Hamstrings, gluteus maximus

**Secondary:** Gluteus medius, lower back extensors

## Golf Focus

The golf world is beginning to appreciate the importance of getting one's body weight onto the target-side leg at impact. The stack and tilt method actually encourages a continuous increase in the weighting of the target leg from the onset of the backswing through the finish of the swing. Positioning the body weight over the target-side leg at impact allows the golfer to drive hard into the ground and explode her pelvis upward, creating a tremendous amount of power development and transfer through the body and into the golf ball. The ability to utilize the large muscles in the hamstrings and buttocks to extend the pelvis is an important aspect of this maneuver. Having proper balance and coordi-

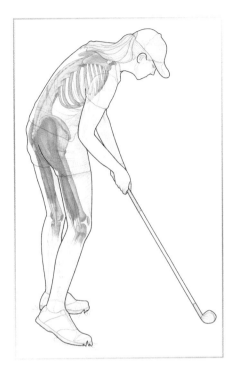

nation in the legs, pelvis, and spine is just as important as having the ability to extend the pelvis. The straight-leg extension variation is a great beginner exercise to develop better pelvis extension as well as coordination and control within the legs, spine, and pelvis.

## VARIATIONS

### Straight-Leg Extension on Stair, Step, or Chair

If you do not have a stability ball or if you are new to exercising and find it difficult to perform the exercise on the stability ball because it keeps rolling away from you, try the same movement but put your heels on a stair, step, or chair. This allows you to strengthen the main movers of this exercise while making it a little easier to balance yourself.

### Unstable Leg Extension on Stability Ball

To make this exercise more challenging, try raising your arms over your chest so that they are reaching up to the ceiling. This will decrease your base of support and force your body to increase the activation of the stabilizing muscles within the pelvis and spine. This is a great way to increase the functional aspect of this exercise.

# Hamstring Curl on Stability Ball

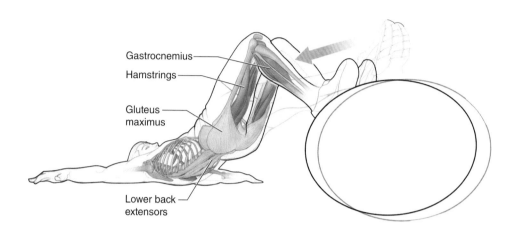

Gastrocnemius

Hamstrings

Gluteus maximus

Lower back extensors

## Execution

1. Lie down with your legs straight and your heels on top of a stability ball.
2. Press down on the ball with your heels and lift your hips.
3. Stay in the lifted position as you bend your knees and roll the ball toward your buttocks.
4. Return your legs to the straight position and repeat.

## Muscles Involved

**Primary:** Hamstrings, gastrocnemius

**Secondary:** Gluteus maximus, lower back extensors

## Golf Focus

One of the significant differences between top professional golfers and the average amateur is the coordination and movement of the legs throughout the golf swing. Many amateurs let the lead leg collapse inward at the knee during the backswing, making it difficult to drive onto the target-side leg during the downswing. When this happens, the golfer will hang back at

impact. This leads to inefficient transfer of energy into the golf ball and
poor direction control of the ball. In
other words, poor leg movement leads
to decreased power and less accuracy.
The hamstring curl on stability ball is
a great exercise to learn how to use
the legs in a coordinated manner and
develop strength along the posterior
chain (calves, hamstrings, glutes, and
lower back extensors). When this
exercise becomes easy, you can try
the modified versions to create more
difficulty and increase the strength in
these muscles. These are great exercises to both develop proper movement within the legs and increase
strength within the hip extensors.

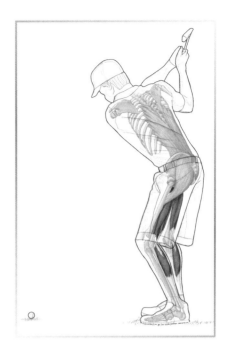

## VARIATIONS

### Unstable Hamstring Curl on Stability Ball

To make this exercise more challenging, try raising your arms over
your chest so that they are reaching up to the ceiling. This will
decrease your base of support and force your body to increase
the activation of the stabilizing muscles within the pelvis and
spine. This is a great way to increase the functional aspect of this
exercise and make it much more challenging.

### One-Leg Hamstring Curl on Stability Ball

When this exercise becomes too easy for you, try the same movement with one leg on the stability ball and the other leg hovering
slightly above the ball. This position will greatly
increase the load on the leg on the ball and
will force the pelvis and spinal stabilizers to work much harder to keep the
pelvis flat and not let it tilt toward
the unsupported side.

# Kneeling Medicine Ball Toss on BOSU Ball

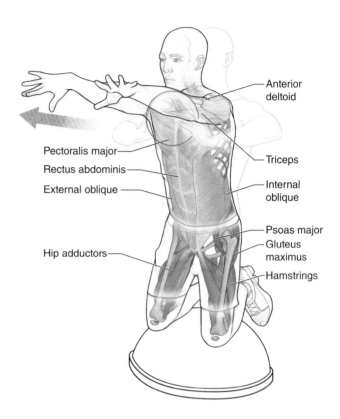

Anterior deltoid

Triceps

Pectoralis major

Rectus abdominis

External oblique

Internal oblique

Psoas major

Gluteus maximus

Hip adductors

Hamstrings

## Execution

1. Kneel on a BOSU ball, dome side up.
2. Raise your feet off the floor.
3. Hold a medicine ball with bent elbows at chest height.
4. Throw the medicine ball to a partner standing in front of you.
5. Catch the ball and repeat.

## Muscles Involved

**Primary:** Hip adductors, psoas major, gluteus maximus, hamstrings

**Secondary:** Pectoralis major, anterior deltoid, triceps, rectus abdominis, external oblique, internal oblique

## Golf Focus

Every golfer has experienced the difficulty of hitting out of the deep rough. Most amateur and many professional golfers have a difficult time maintaining their balance when they attempt to put a little extra muscular effort into the shot while trying to power the ball out of the rough. Often they will extend early from their posture and will not be able to drive through the thick grass to make solid contact with the ball. This is due to both a weakness in their ability to stabilize the body and poor balance and proprioception in the spine and pelvis. The kneeling medicine ball toss on BOSU ball will help train balance and stability at the same time, making it a great option for players of all levels.

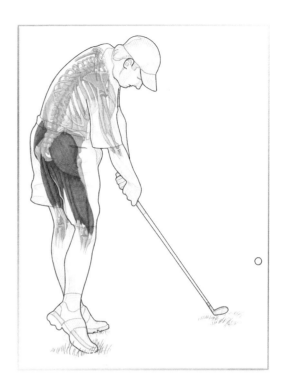

### VARIATION

### Kneeling Medicine Ball Toss on Stability Ball

When your balance improves on the BOSU ball and your stabilization and strength get to the point where the BOSU ball version of this exercise becomes easy, you can try the same exercise on a stability ball. This makes the balance aspect much more difficult.

# Tug of War

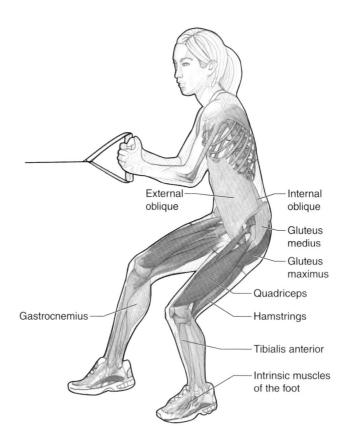

## Execution

1. Stand on one leg, and hold onto the handle of exercise tubing with one or two hands. If using one hand, place the other hand on your abdomen.
2. Have a partner hold onto the other handle and attempt to pull you off your one leg. Your partner can be standing on one leg or on both legs.
3. Perform the desired number of repetitions and repeat with the opposite leg.

## Muscles Involved

**Primary:** Intrinsic muscles of the foot, quadriceps, hamstrings, gluteus maximus

**Secondary:** Internal oblique, external oblique, tibialis anterior, gluteus medius, gastrocnemius

## Golf Focus

There is something majestic about watching a golfer who develops a great deal of power from the legs and has the stability and balance to transfer that power through the body and into the ball at impact while remaining in perfect balance into the follow-through. Anthony Kim is a young player who exhibits such a skill. Having great balance and strength in your legs allows you to drive through the ball onto your target side at impact and into a well-balanced follow-through. The tug of war exercise is a fun way to improve your balance and increase the strength of your legs simultaneously.

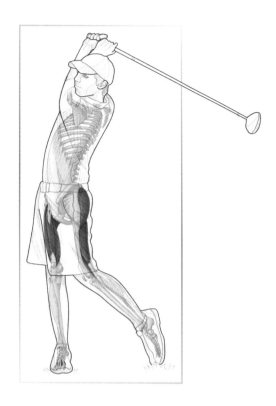

## VARIATIONS

### Tug of War With Eyes Closed

To make the balance aspect much more difficult and really work the small muscles and ligaments in your foot and ankle, try this exercise with your eyes closed. Make sure your partner doesn't pull too hard, though! Closing the eyes and having to stabilize in random multiple directions places a lot of stress on the receptors of your foot. This makes them develop quicker for better results on the course.

### Tug of War With One Foot on BOSU Ball

When your balance and strength have improved to the point where tug of war becomes easy for you, try performing the same exercise while standing on the flat side of a BOSU ball. This creates an unstable platform for you to balance on and places even more responsibility on the small muscles in your foot to provide quick and accurate information as to where your body weight is in reference to your foot and what muscles need to be stabilized in order to maintain your balance.

# Knee-Up Reverse Lunge

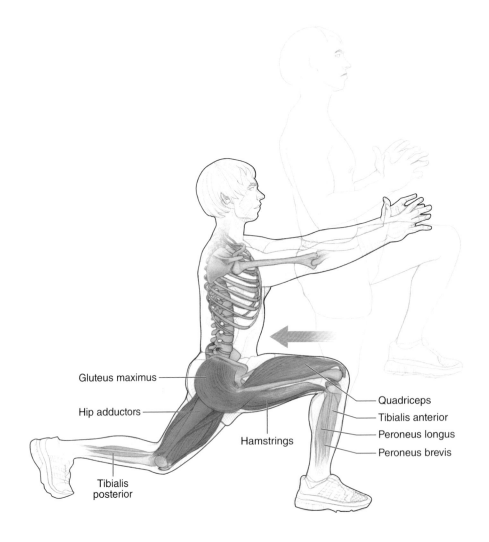

Gluteus maximus

Hip adductors

Hamstrings

Tibialis posterior

Quadriceps

Tibialis anterior

Peroneus longus

Peroneus brevis

## Execution

1. Stand on your right leg with your left knee bent 90 degrees and left thigh parallel to the ground.
2. Reach your left leg straight back behind you, and touch your foot to the ground.
3. Drop your left knee straight down, and barely touch it to the ground.
4. Push through your right heel, and return to the start position.
5. Perform the desired number of repetitions and repeat with the opposite leg.

## Muscles Involved

**Primary:** Gluteus maximus, quadriceps, hip adductors, hamstrings

**Secondary:** Tibialis anterior, tibialis posterior, peroneus longus, peroneus brevis

## Golf Focus

This is a great exercise to not only challenge your balance but also gain some strength in your legs. Keeping proper form is crucial in order to work the muscles properly and get the most efficient results. Keep most of your weight on your front heel while going into the reverse lunge as well as coming up from it. This allows your glutes to activate as much as possible. Also, the foot that you step back with should only lightly touch the ground. This forces you to keep the weight on your front heel and challenges your balance as much as possible. The knee-up reverse lunge gives you the strength, balance, and muscle control you will need for shots that require a little extra power.

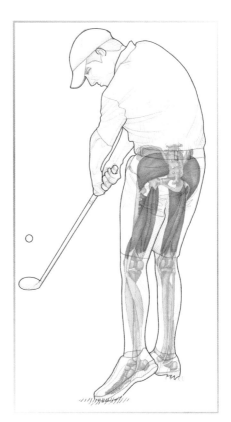

---

### VARIATION

## Walking Knee-Up Lunge

For a slightly easier version of this exercise, perform walking lunges in a forward direction. Continue to bring one knee up in between lunges to challenge balance. This works the same muscles but requires a little less control and balance to perform.

# STRENGTH FOR FATIGUE-FREE GOLF

**W**hen we speak about strength in golf, we are talking about a complex, multifaceted concept. There is no definitive list of characteristics that identify the "strongest" golfers. We see many of today's top golfers on a daily basis within the confines of the PGA Tour fitness trailers, and there is definitely a large range in their individual physical skill sets.

What is obvious, however, is that those players who are "golf strong" have higher than average performance in a number of individual fitness categories. These categories include balance, body awareness, stability, neuromuscular coordination, power, and endurance. When a golfer is below average in any one of these skill sets, the resultant functional weakness becomes apparent in the golf swing.

Golfers can be above average in strength in the gym while training with machines or free weights, but if they are not able to transfer that gym strength to the golf course, they are wasting the time they spend on their fitness. Traditional bodybuilding has little to no place in developing a strong body for golf. Bodybuilders are concerned about how much weight they can move during an exercise as well as the size of their individual muscles. As a golfer, you need to work your body through multiple planes of movement while concentrating on creating the proper sequencing of muscle activation (using the correct muscles in the correct order during each exercise). We are not saying that muscle strength does not matter, but if the individual muscles cannot communicate and work with each other, then that strength will be useless in your golf swing. For this reason, it is crucial to formulate your fitness routine with exercises that not only improve individual muscle strength but also improve the way muscles work together. This is what we mean by creating functional strength and not just raw strength (figure 5.1).

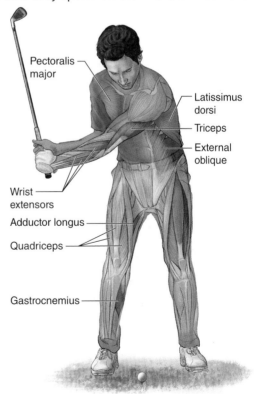

**Figure 5.1** Functional strength requires muscles to communicate with each other throughout the swing.

To be truly golf strong, you need to have strength through the entire range of motion involved during your golf swing. A weakness at any joint through any section of the motion will create a breakdown in your golf swing. Lifting weights in one plane while using a bench or traditional machines greatly limits the functional strength that you can develop. This approach eliminates the need for your body to create and maintain stabilization through a full range of motion while performing an exercise. This ability to stabilize is exactly what is needed in golf and therefore must be heavily incorporated into your exercise routine. You will then see that the strength you gain in your fitness training begins to have a much greater carryover to the golf course. For this reason, we have formulated this chapter on golf strength to include exercises that expand on movements and concepts described in the previous chapters and combine them into more functional movements. The exercises in this chapter should be performed only when the exercises in the balance, stability, and mobility chapters can be completed comfortably and with good form.

Many people think that golfers do not need to be strong since they are not running, jumping, or knocking other people over. This attitude is probably due to the fact that the word *strength* typically conjures up images of a guy with huge muscles benching 300 pounds (135 kg) in the gym. Although this is one form of strength, there are many others. We have already explained that golfers require more of a *functional* strength to perform at the highest levels. There is also another key reason that strength is important: injury prevention.

The average person would never associate the two words *golf* and *injury*. However, as all professional golfers and avid amateur players know, injuries are prevalent throughout the sport and in fact are almost inevitable. The statistics on injuries at the touring level are staggering. About half of all touring professional golfers will have some injury each year that will cause them to miss many weeks of golf. Of those that are playing, up to 30 percent are actually playing injured. Those numbers are very high, and any single injury in a given year can be the difference between keeping your playing card or not. For touring professionals, the tour card is their job ticket. Lose the card, lose the job. For nonprofessional golfers, an injury may mean missing many months of golf or, even worse, deciding to quit golf altogether. For these reasons alone, you should increase your golf strength so you can prevent injuries as much as possible.

You may still be wondering how strength and injuries relate. Let us explain. First of all, there are mainly two types of injuries that occur in golf: joint injuries and soft tissue (muscles, tendons, and ligaments) injuries. Although there are no heavy loads to carry or move in golf (unless you are a caddy!), very high forces develop because of the speed of the swing. The muscles and joints not only help to create these forces but also must be able to generate opposite forces to slow down and ultimately stop the swing. As muscle strength—both individual and functional—increases, so does your ability to withstand the forces within the golf swing. If you do not possess adequate strength in the muscles to create and slow down these forces, then injury is sure to occur. Your soft tissues are your first layer of protection, but when the strength in these soft tissues cannot control the speed and rotation of the swing, the joints will begin to absorb the energy. Although the joints are capable of withstanding some force, they cannot be asked to be the major contributor to acceleration and deceleration. This scenario will surely cause injury and make it impossible to create an efficient swing. Therefore, building up your strength not only helps with your golf swing but also helps ensure you can take as many golf swings as you like.

By properly implementing the exercises in this chapter into your exercise program, you will see rapid improvement in both your confidence and physical competence in your golf swing. As an added bonus, it will also help you avoid taking time off because of injuries, which would slow down the progression of your game. As your success with these exercises improves, so will the ease with which you are able to control your body on the course. Become *functionally strong* and you will become *golf strong*!

For the following exercises, perform 8 to 12 repetitions. For exercises that require resistance tubing, cable machines, or free weights, start with a low resistance that allows you to complete 3 sets of 12 repetitions per set. When you can complete 3 sets of 12 repetitions, increase the resistance or weight so you can complete 11 repetitions but struggle on the last one. For exercises that require only body weight, begin with 2 or 3 sets of 8 repetitions. Once you can easily complete 3 sets of 8 repetitions, increase to 10 repetitions. Some exercises may require other ranges of repetitions. In these cases, the number of sets and repetitions is included with the exercise instruction.

# Side-to-Side Walk With Tubing

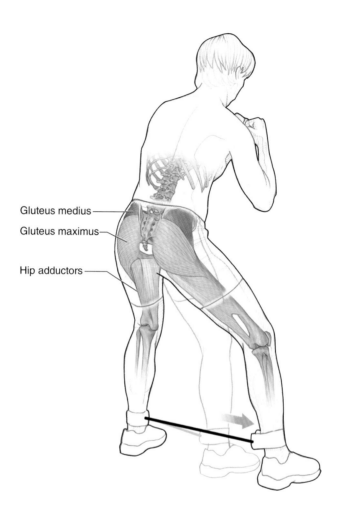

Gluteus medius
Gluteus maximus
Hip adductors

## Execution

1. Place ankle cuffs with tubing on both ankles.
2. Stand with feet shoulder-width apart, slightly bend your hips and knees, keep your back straight, and keep your feet pointing straight forward.
3. Step toward the right as far as you can, keeping your feet pointing forward and your back straight.
4. Slowly bring your left leg to the right to achieve the start position once again.
5. Repeat the desired number of repetitions, and then walk to the left to return to the start.

## Muscles Involved

**Primary:** Gluteus medius, gluteus minimus

**Secondary:** Gluteus maximus, hip adductors

## Golf Focus

As linear and rotational speeds increase in the swing, it is important to have enough strength to withstand these forces. The muscles in your hips need to not only generate hip rotation but also be strong enough to slow down rotation and stabilize the hips. This keeps your hips from swaying away from the target on the backswing and sliding toward the target on the downswing. These two swing faults are very common and many times are due to lack of strength in the hip muscles. This exercise will help you strengthen the hip muscles that keep you rotating around your hips instead of swaying and sliding. During the exercise, move slowly to avoid using momentum, and keep your feet pointed forward at all times. To increase the difficulty, use tubing with more resistance.

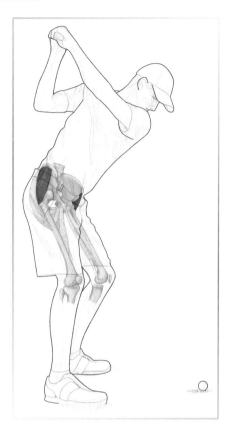

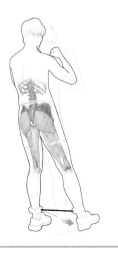

## VARIATION

### Standing Hip Abductor With Tubing

This exercise will work the same muscles but can be slightly more challenging. You will be working the muscles of the leg you are lifting, plus your stance leg will be working very hard to keep you balanced and stationary. Try to keep your torso as still as possible during the movement.

# Plié Squat

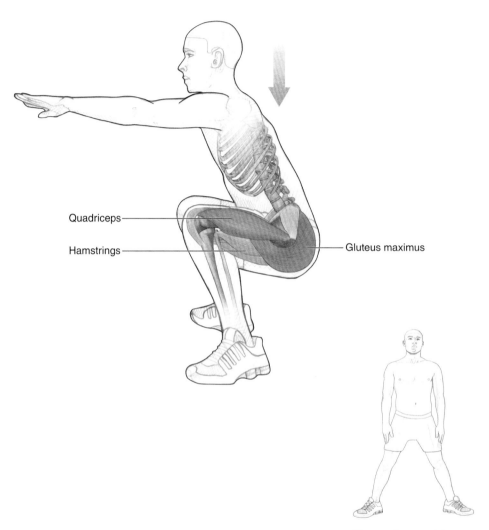

Quadriceps

Hamstrings

Gluteus maximus

**Alternative position.**

## Execution

1. Stand with your legs wider than your shoulders and your feet turned outward 45 degrees.
2. Lower your butt backward and down while raising your arms forward to shoulder height.
3. Maintain a straight back in the lowered position with your knees over your feet (don't collapse the knees inward as you lower).
4. Attempt to lower yourself so your thighs are parallel to the ground.
5. Perform the desired number of repetitions.

## Muscles Involved

**Primary:** Quadriceps, gluteus maximus

**Secondary:** Hip adductors, hamstrings

## Golf Focus

One of the components of any good golf swing is having the leg strength to transfer body weight onto the lead leg and to extend the hips up through impact. This move creates a tremendous amount of force to be applied against the ground, which in turn is applied back into the golfer by the ground. This is the initial step in creating power within a golf swing. The plié squat is a safe movement for almost anyone beginning a leg exercise program to develop this strength. Externally rotating the feet makes it easier to move the hips through the lowered position and applies less stress to the knees.

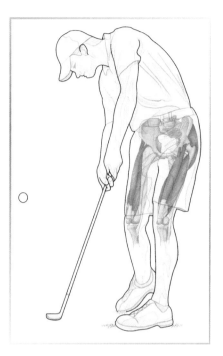

## VARIATION

### Plié Squat With Weight

Some of you may find it difficult to keep your hips back as you lower toward the ground. When this happens, it is often easier to use both hands to hold a *light* weight of no more than 20 pounds. As you push your hips backward during the squat motion, you can lift the weight up to shoulder height to maintain balance by keeping your center of mass within your base of support (between your feet). This is an example of how a little weight added to an exercise can actually make the movement easier.

# Seated Row With Tubing

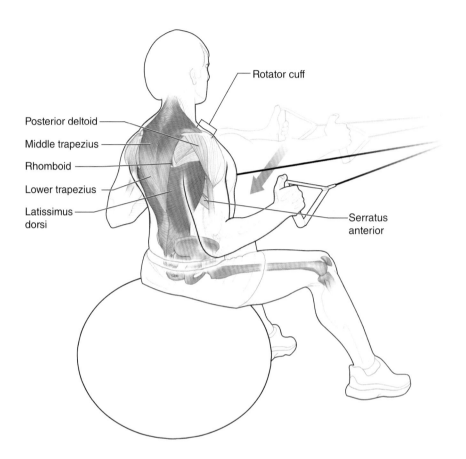

## Execution

1. Wrap tubing around a stationary object, and hold onto a handle in each hand. Sit on a stability ball with your back straight, knees bent, and heels on the floor.
2. With your elbows straight, lightly squeeze your shoulder blades together and down, and hold this throughout the exercise. This is your start position.
3. Keep your body steady as you slowly bend your elbows and move them toward your sides.
4. Return to the start position.
5. Repeat the desired number of repetitions.

## Muscles Involved

**Primary:** Rhomboid, middle trapezius, latissimus dorsi

**Secondary:** Serratus anterior, lower trapezius, posterior deltoid, rotator cuff

## Golf Focus

As mentioned in the stability chapter, it is important to have proper control of the shoulder blades. When a golfer is able to pull his shoulder blade in toward his spine and away from his ear, it places the shoulder complex in a position that is advantageous for the proper functioning of the latissimus dorsi muscle. When the latissimus dorsi (the muscle that looks like a wing on a bodybuilder) is able to pull forcefully, it will help drive the golfer onto his target leg through the downswing. As we all know, the more you are on your target-side leg at impact, the greater you can drive your legs into the ground, which all combines to produce greater club-head speed. When a golfer does not control his target shoulder properly, it will usually pop up toward his ear at

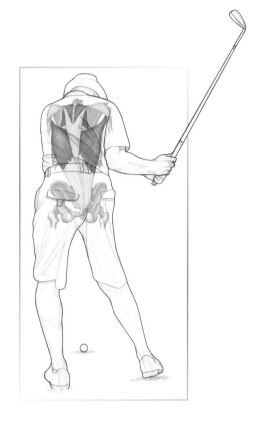

the beginning of the downswing, which forces the golfer's upper body back onto his trail leg throughout the downswing and contact phases of the golf swing. This will not allow for good transfer of weight to the target leg and will put more stress on the lower back as the golfer hangs back through impact.

---

### VARIATION

### Seated Row With Cable

If you are at a gym, you can perform this exercise on a cable machine that is designed for a seated row. The advantage of using a cable machine over tubing is that the tension remains constant throughout the entire range of motion (as compared with the increased resistance experienced as tubing stretches). Just be careful to leave your ego at the door and use good form. It is common to see people crank up the weight as soon as they get on this machine, which is a surefire route to bad form and an injury! If you cannot hold your shoulder blades in place during the entire exercise, you are using too much weight.

# Diagonal Triceps Extension

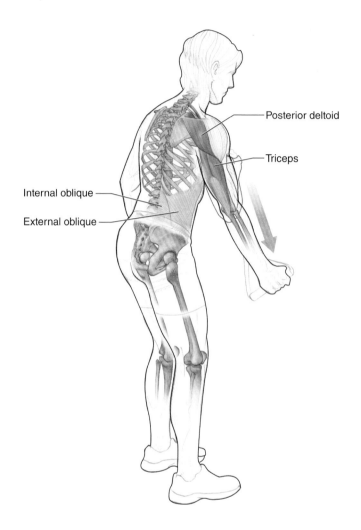

Posterior deltoid

Triceps

Internal oblique

External oblique

## Execution

1. Stand in your golf setup posture. With your right hand, grab a resistance band that is attached above your head and to the left.
2. Start with your elbow fully bent and pointed just out in front of your right toes.
3. Straighten your elbow without moving your upper arm, and pull the resistance band down toward the ground.
4. Return slowly to the start position without moving your upper arm, and repeat.
5. Perform the desired number of repetitions and repeat on the opposite side.

## Muscles Involved

**Primary:** Triceps, posterior deltoid

**Secondary:** Internal oblique, external oblique

## Golf Focus

It is very important to be able to create and hold angles within the golf swing. However, holding these angles, or creating lag, is beneficial only if you can release them efficiently. As the lower body begins the downswing, the arms and wrists must maintain their angles to increase potential power. As the downswing continues, these angles must be released effectively to pass the energy from the torso to the arms and then to the club. The diagonal triceps extension will strengthen the muscles that transfer the energy from your torso to your arms and prepare it to enter the club. Increasing the strength in these muscles allows you to create more lag and therefore more power in your swing. This method of exercising the triceps also strengthens the oblique muscles as you resist rotation from the weight.

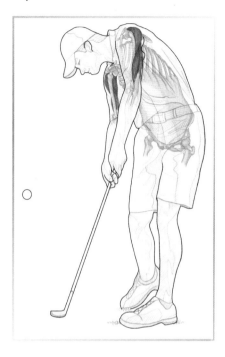

---

### VARIATION

### Diagonal Triceps Extension With Cable

This same exercise can be done when you have access to a gym and a cable machine. Use a handle strap attached to a high cable machine. Perform the same movements as with the resistance band. This will be more difficult because the weight remains constant throughout the entire exercise. Increase the resistance only if you can keep good form for each repetition.

# Straight-Arm Pull-Down

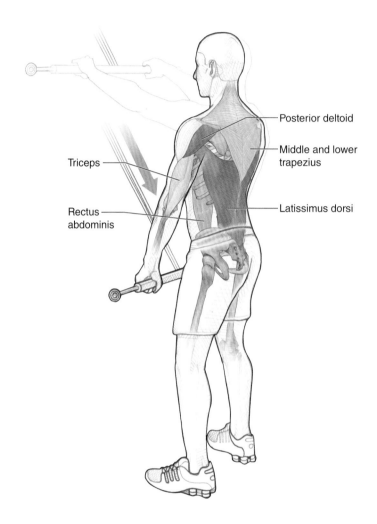

Posterior deltoid

Middle and lower trapezius

Triceps

Latissimus dorsi

Rectus abdominis

## Execution

1. On a high cable machine, take a wide grip on a lat bar.
2. Keep your shoulders down and back and your elbows locked.
3. Pull the bar down until your arms are near your sides.
4. Slowly return to the start position.

## Muscles Involved

**Primary:** Latissimus dorsi, posterior deltoid

**Secondary:** Rectus abdominis, triceps, middle trapezius, lower trapezius

## Golf Focus

The latissimus dorsi muscle needs to have efficient mobility in order to make a comfortable and efficient backswing. However, it is also important to be able to use the tremendous power available within this large muscle. This exercise helps isolate the latissimus dorsi as well as trains your ability to stabilize your body against outside force. When the club reaches the top of the backswing, the hips start to change direction to begin the downswing. At this point the latissimus dorsi muscle is fully lengthened. The stretch of the muscle puts it in a perfect position to quickly shorten and produce power as energy is transferred from the hips to the upper body. So once you gain mobility in the latissimus dorsi muscle, you must be able to shorten it effectively. This exercise will not only help you gain that strength but also help you gain control of the muscle as you stabilize your body against the resistance.

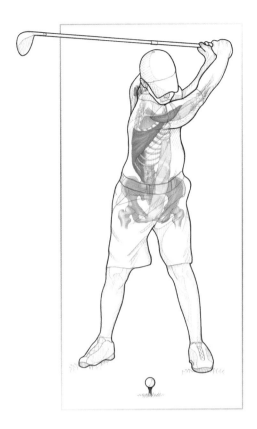

## VARIATIONS

### One-Leg Straight-Arm Pull-Down

To challenge your balance simultaneously, perform the same exercise while standing on one foot. This will force you to stabilize greatly in order to pull the cable bar downward. Be aware that you may have to decrease the weight to perform the exercise correctly.

### One-Arm Pull-Down

This version will also work your obliques. As you pull the weight down, you have to resist your body's natural tendency to rotate. This is a great way to mimic how the body works during the swing: One body part moves while another stabilizes.

# Reverse Push-Up

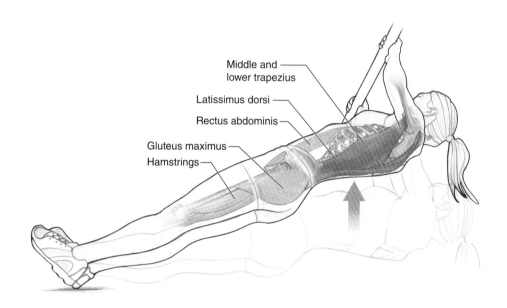

## Execution

1. Lie on your back underneath the bar on a Smith machine.
2. Take a wide grip on the bar and hang so that your body is completely straight, slightly off the ground, and supported by your heels.
3. Keeping your body straight, pull yourself toward the bar so that the bar reaches midchest.
4. Return slowly to the start position and repeat.

## Muscles Involved

**Primary:** Latissimus dorsi, middle trapezius, lower trapezius

**Secondary:** Rectus abdominis, gluteus maximus, hamstrings

## Golf Focus

As you move into extreme ranges of motions within the golf swing, it becomes more difficult to maintain proper body angles and correct posture. As you perform this exercise, it is very important to keep your body completely straight and to create the movement with the muscles in your back. This will strengthen your abdominal muscles (as they resist the tendency of your hips to fall toward the ground) as well as the muscles of your upper and middle back. These back muscles need to have the strength to maintain proper spinal posture when you are in full backswing. Without this strength, your upper back will want to begin rounding, and your shoulders will want to roll forward. This loss of posture in the backswing can make it nearly impossible to get the club back on path in the down-

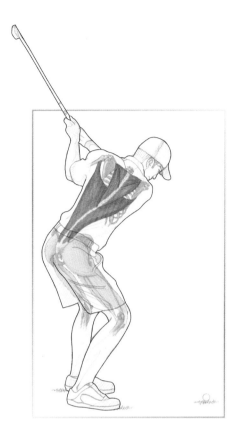

swing and return the club face square for impact. Reverse push-ups will help prevent this costly swing fault and give you the strength you need to maintain proper posture.

---

### VARIATION

### Assisted Pull-Up

If reverse push-ups are too difficult to do correctly, try the assisted version. However, you must have access to an assisted pull-up machine. The assisted pull-up focuses more directly on the latissimus dorsi muscle. Keep your shoulders down and back as much as possible, and focus on pulling with your back muscles.

# Half Side Plank Hip Series

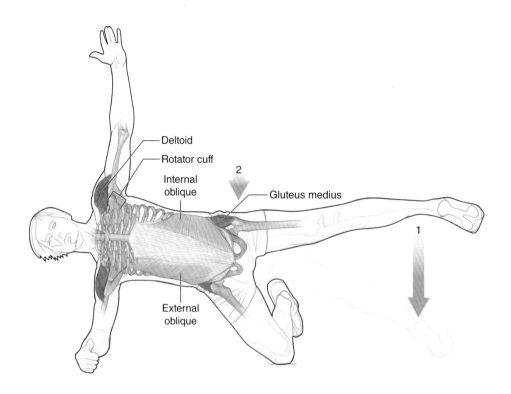

## Execution

1. Lie sideways so that you are supported by your right forearm and knee. The left leg is in the air and parallel to the ground. Your body should be in a straight line from head to hip to foot of the top leg. Bend your bottom knee to 90 degrees.

2. Hold for 10 seconds.

3. Lower the left leg to the floor, return to parallel, and repeat 2 to 10 times.

4. Return the left leg to the air and hold it there. Lower the right hip 1 inch (2.5 cm) toward the ground; don't move at the shoulder. Lift the hip up again and repeat until you complete the desired number of repetitions.

5. Repeat on the other side.

## Muscles Involved

**Primary:** Gluteus medius, deltoid

**Secondary:** Rotator cuff, internal oblique, external oblique

## Golf Focus

One of the main problems amateur golfers have is not being able to drive hard onto their target side through the downswing. They also lack sufficient hip rotation and the ability to stabilize the pelvis at impact without sliding toward the target. This move requires a tremendous amount of strength in the hip and pelvic stabilizers. The half side plank hip series is a great exercise to develop strength throughout the entire pelvic region. When these movements become easier in the gym, you will definitely notice more stability as you move through the ball on the course.

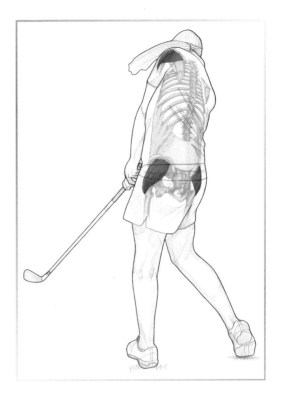

### VARIATION

## Side Leg Lift Using a Bench

If you have shoulder or neck pain, try modifying this exercise by placing your bottom forearm on top of a bench. This will help take the load off the shoulder and put the neck in an easier position for those with weak neck muscles or neck discomfort.

# Reverse Squatting Woodchop
# With Medicine Ball

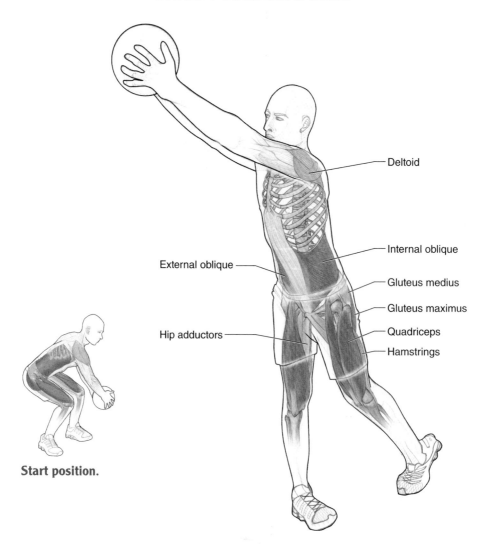

Deltoid

Internal oblique

External oblique

Gluteus medius

Gluteus maximus

Quadriceps

Hip adductors

Hamstrings

**Start position.**

## Execution

1. Get in a squat position, and hold a medicine ball in both hands.
2. Reach the ball toward the outside of your left ankle.
3. Stand up while simultaneously rotating to your right and lifting the ball overhead.
4. Finish with your right foot in place, your body rotated around your right hip, and the medicine ball up and to the right.
5. Perform the desired number of repetitions, and repeat in the other direction.

## Muscles Involved

**Primary:** Gluteus maximus, quadriceps, internal oblique, external oblique

**Secondary:** Deltoid, gluteus medius, hamstrings, hip adductors

## Golf Focus

The importance of rotational movements in golf is very obvious. To achieve an efficient and powerful golf swing, all muscles involved must be conditioned and strengthened. However, having strong muscles does not mean you will automatically be able to use them in the correct order. The reverse squatting woodchop is a great exercise to strengthen these muscles on an individual level as well as in conjunction with each other. As you begin this exercise, you will notice that it is much easier to perform if you allow the strength and energy from your lower body to pass to your upper body as you rotate upward. As you become better at this movement, you will be able to use more weight and perform more repetitions. This occurs not because of increased strength alone, but also because your body has learned how to perform a complex rotational

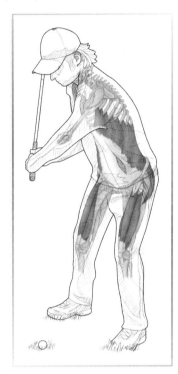

movement more efficiently. This is exactly what is needed in each and every golf swing, especially those you have to perform from an awkward stance and lie while still powerfully getting the club under the ball.

---

### VARIATION

## Reverse Squatting Woodchop With Cable

Using a cable machine to do this exercise will help you train the same muscles. However, you will find that it is a little more awkward to control the movement because of the nature of the cable. This will help to more effectively train the muscles that stabilize the motion.

# Push-Up to Plank

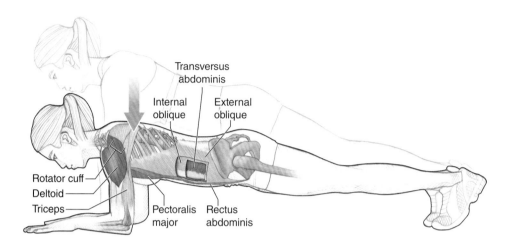

## Execution

1. Start in a push-up position with your hands directly under your shoulders.
2. Lower yourself one arm at a time until your weight is supported by your forearms and toes (like the plank).
3. Try not to have much side-to-side hip movement through the transitions.
4. Return to the start position by pushing up one arm at a time.
5. Perform the desired number of repetitions.

## Muscles Involved

**Primary:** Deltoid, pectoralis major, rectus abdominis, transversus abdominis

**Secondary:** Triceps, internal oblique, external oblique, rotator cuff

## Golf Focus

Every golfer has felt the disappointment of walking down the fairway after hitting a wonderful tee shot to find that the ball has run just through the fairway and is now lying in thick rough. It's a short-iron shot to a hard green, and a little spin on the ball sure would help keep the ball relatively close to the flag. These approach shots are done easily by players such as Anthony Kim, Hunter Mahan, and Tiger Woods. Why? Well, besides having exceptional technique, they are also very functionally strong from their feet right through their legs, core, shoulders, and arms. They are able to drive through the rough without losing much club-head speed or club stability and still create enough ball compression to

generate some spin on the ball as it exits. The push-up to plank is a difficult exercise to do properly, but it will help generate strength from the pelvis and through the core, shoulders, and arms.

---

## VARIATION

### Push-Up to Plank From Knees

If you do not have the strength to do this exercise from your toes, you can try modifying it by keeping your knees on the ground. This is a great version for golfers just learning this movement.

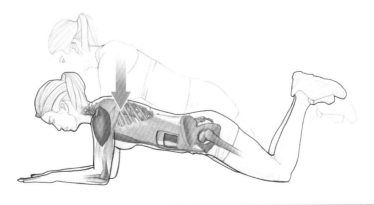

# One-Leg Reaching Squat

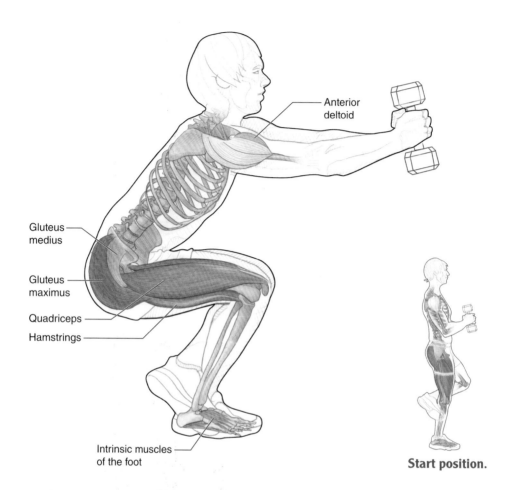

Anterior deltoid

Gluteus medius

Gluteus maximus

Quadriceps

Hamstrings

Intrinsic muscles of the foot

**Start position.**

## Execution

1. Stand with your left ankle crossed behind the right calf.
2. Bend both knees as you squat by pushing your buttocks behind you.
3. As you bend your knees, extend both arms up to shoulder height for balance.
4. Slowly stand up out of the squat by pushing the hips forward.
5. Do the necessary repetitions, and switch legs.

## Muscles Involved

**Primary:** Gluteus maximus, quadriceps, hamstrings

**Secondary:** Intrinsic muscles of the foot, gluteus medius, hip adductors, anterior deltoid

## Golf Focus

There are many situations on the golf course where strength and balance are required to make a quality golf shot. In this image, you will notice the golfer attempting to hit a ball from the rough with the ball lying below his feet. This is a great example of a golf shot requiring tremendous body control and strength to pull off consistently. When a golfer does not possess these attributes, there is often too much movement through the impact zone, and good shots become more a matter of chance than good technique. The one-leg reaching squat is a great exercise to build both functional leg and core strength while simultaneously requiring a tremendous amount of stability and balance. This exercise won't guarantee that you will make these difficult golf shots every time, but it should increase your chances of success.

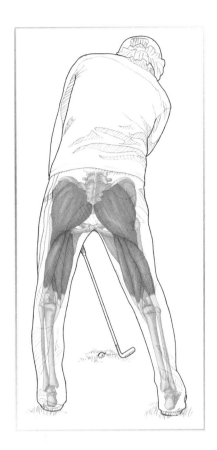

---

### VARIATION

### Supported One-Leg Squat

To make this exercise a little less demanding, you can try holding onto a railing or door knob with both hands. This allows you to concentrate less on balance and more on proper positioning of your body as you push the hips backward to lower into the squat and push the hips forward to rise out of the squat. As you get more comfortable, try putting less and less weight on the railing until you can do the movement with no support at all.

# EXPLOSIVE POWER FOR LONGER DRIVES

**G**olf is often thought of as an easy game played by wealthy older adults. It is not often perceived by the public as a sport requiring explosive, complex, and difficult movements. This unfortunate perspective could not be further from the truth. The golf swing is one of the most dynamic movements in all of sport. The explosion of speed experienced by the world's greatest golfers during the swing is unparalleled in other sports. Let's consider the extremely small period of time that passes from when a golfer reaches the top of his backswing (figure 6.1) to when he has performed the downswing, made contact with the ball, and then decelerated the golf club at the completion of the follow-through. Approximately .20 seconds. Yes, one-fifth of a second. That is the amount of time it takes a golfer to accelerate the club from 0 miles per hour at the top of the backswing to more than 100 miles per hour (160 km/h) at impact and then back to 0 miles per hour at the end of the golf swing.

Before we go any further, we should consider the definition of power. Power is work divided by time. Knowing that time is a key component of the power formula, it is easy to see that few movements in sport are as truly powerful as an elite-level golf swing. If we look at some of the more popular and explosive players on the PGA Tour, such as Tiger Woods, Phil Mickelson, Anthony Kim, Hunter Mahan, Dustin Johnson, and Sean O'Hair, we see six very different bodies. The one common thread that ties these players together and allows each of them to regularly hit the ball well in excess of 300 yards is not pure strength. It is the ability to perform movements very, very quickly. Not only can these golfers create movement, specifically the golf swing, very quickly, but they can also get up to these high speeds almost instantaneously.

One of the problems with traditional fitness training for golf is

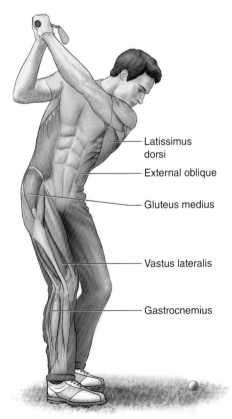

Latissimus dorsi

External oblique

Gluteus medius

Vastus lateralis

Gastrocnemius

**Figure 6.1** Golfer at the top of the backswing.

that it doesn't include explosive movements. Most trainers don't consider the highly explosive nature of the golf swing when thinking about golf fitness. Instead, they consider golf a sport in which all you need to be able to do is to walk four to six hours while playing. However, in this book we not only want you to understand why power is important to golf, but we also want to show you how it can be trained effectively and transferred directly to your golf swing (figure 6.2).

A prerequisite for power training is to develop the skill sets from the preceding chapters. This is why we have designed this book so that the functional exercises are in a specific chapter order. For almost every exercise in the power chapter, there is a definite need for balance, stability, mobility, and strength. Therefore, these must all be trained before attempting the movements that develop power. This

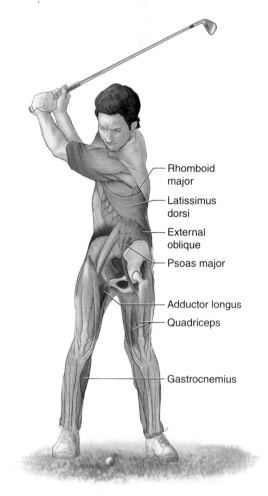

Figure 6.2    The golf swing is an explosive movement.

will not only help you avoid injury but also make your power training more effective. We have devoted this chapter to the golfing athletes who want to take their bodies to the highest level and achieve explosive capabilities. We have included various training modalities, including upper body and lower body plyometrics as well as short power movements utilizing medicine balls, tubing, and body weight. Remember that power by definition requires movements to be quick and not necessarily performed with heavy weight. We are more concerned about proper technique coupled with speed of movement than we are with the amount of weight being moved.

Another thing you need to understand is that power training is not necessarily designed to build large muscles. Strength training programs are often more successful at obtaining those results. Power training programs, on the other hand, will help train the body's nervous system to react faster. This allows for a more rapid transmission of information through the body, which leads to a quicker and more explosive reaction to stress. This is exactly what you need in the golf swing (figure 6.3). When reaction time is trained, improved, and controlled, it can produce massive power and longer ball flight. Consider the physique of sprinter Usain Bolt and his phenomenal success in the 100 meters. It is easy to see that you can become extremely explosive and powerful and not look like a bodybuilder.

Although hitting longer is a dream of many golfers, there are many aspects involved in gaining true, useful power in the golf swing. It is not all about one facet of fitness; it's about creating a solid foundation on which power can be built. Even if you do train correctly and have a body fit for golf, you must always be cautious when training with speed because injuries can be more prevalent. For this reason, it is very important that you warm up before doing power exercises. We suggest doing multiple movements in which you move all body parts, muscles, and joints through a *full* range of motion. Begin each movement slowly and within small ranges of motion, and gradually increase both the

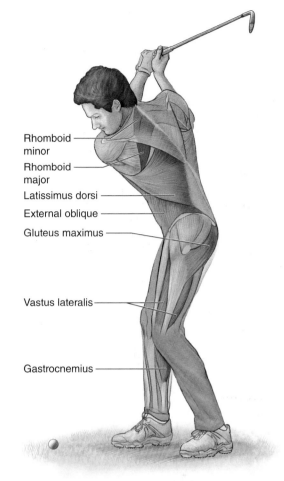

Rhomboid minor
Rhomboid major
Latissimus dorsi
External oblique
Gluteus maximus

Vastus lateralis

Gastrocnemius

**Figure 6.3** Power training leads to faster reactions and more explosive movements.

speed and motion. Your goal is not only to get your body loose and used to going through full ranges of motions but also to actually warm up your body so that the muscles are better prepared to both move and protect. Properly warming up does take a little bit more time, but it pays off by helping to keep you on the course and out of the doctor's office.

Unless otherwise noted, perform 8 to 12 repetitions of the exercises in this chapter. For exercises that require resistance tubing, a cable machine, or free weights, start with a low resistance or weight that enables you to complete 3 sets of 12 repetitions per set. Once you can complete 3 sets of 12 repetitions, increase the weight until you can perform 11 repetitions but struggle on the last one. For exercises that use body weight only, begin with 2 or 3 sets of 8 repetitions and increase to 10 repetitions once you can easily complete 3 sets of 8.

Although any exercise can be dangerous if not performed properly, exercises designed to create power are often more strenuous on the body and should be performed under the supervision of an experienced fitness professional and after gaining medical clearance. If you experience any discomfort while performing these movements, consult a qualified professional for guidance.

# Deadlift With Barbell

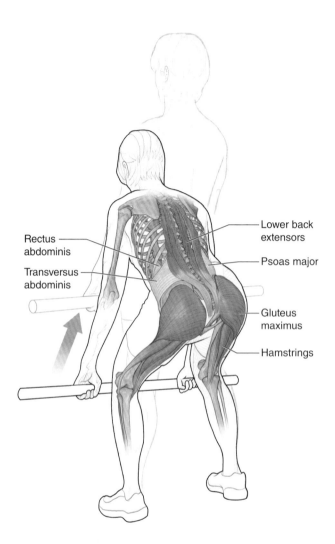

Rectus abdominis

Transversus abdominis

Lower back extensors

Psoas major

Gluteus maximus

Hamstrings

## Execution

1. Stand with feet slightly more than shoulder-width apart while holding a barbell. Use a weight that allows you to complete 8 to 12 repetitions with good form.
2. Keep your knees bent, back straight, and weight on your heels.
3. Begin by moving your hips backward and then bending forward at the waist.
4. Go down until the barbell is below your knees.
5. Return to the start position by pushing through the heels and moving your hips forward.

## Muscles Involved

**Primary:** Gluteus maximus, hamstrings, lower back extensors

**Secondary:** Rectus abdominis, transversus abdominis, psoas major

## Golf Focus

The deadlift is a very important movement to be able to perform. This movement pattern ensures that the proper muscles are working any time you need to bend over at the waist. In the golf swing, you must be able to utilize your glutes and hamstrings not only to support and stabilize your lower body through the backswing but also to generate power in transition to the downswing. This exercise will help you learn how to both move efficiently and use the strength of the glutes and hamstrings without placing excessive stress on the lower back. This is crucial for your golf swing so that you can create as much power as possible while staying away from positions and movements that will increase your risk of injury. Keep your back straight throughout the entire exercise so that all movement comes from your hips.

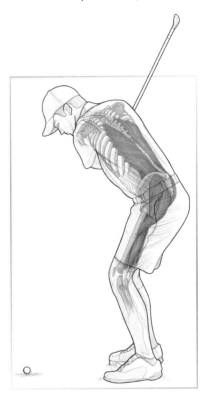

---

**VARIATION**

### Deadlift With Cable

Perform this same exercise on a cable machine. However, make sure to maintain resistance during the entire movement. Do not let the weight stack rest when you get into the lower position of the deadlift.

# Lateral Bounding

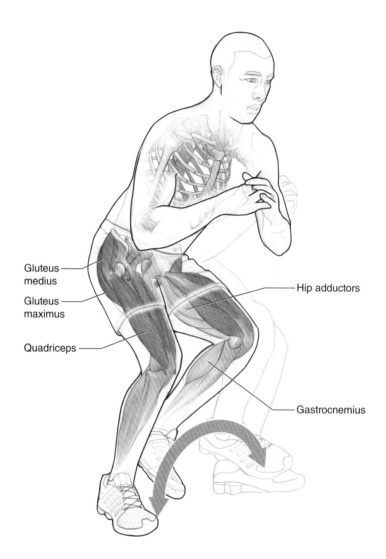

Gluteus medius

Gluteus maximus

Quadriceps

Hip adductors

Gastrocnemius

## Execution

1. Stand mostly on your right foot with your knees slightly bent.
2. Jump to your left 3 to 5 feet (.9 to 1.5 m).
3. Land on your left foot with your knee slightly bent. Do not allow your hip or torso to move to the outside of your left foot.
4. Repeat, jumping to the right. Perform the desired number of repetitions.

## Muscles Involved

**Primary:** Gluteus medius, gluteus maximus, quadriceps

**Secondary:** Gastrocnemius, hip adductors

## Golf Focus

The creation of power within the golf swing comes from your ability to generate speed from the ground all the way to the club head. Transferring this energy efficiently allows you to hit the ball with all the power you create during the backswing and downswing. As you move into the transition phase of the swing, power is generated as weight distribution shifts to your lead leg. Your lower body initiates this power drive, and once you stabilize your hips, this same energy is transferred up the chain until it eventually reaches the club head. This exercise will help you generate more power from your lower body as well as stabilize more effectively to make sure that all the energy you create

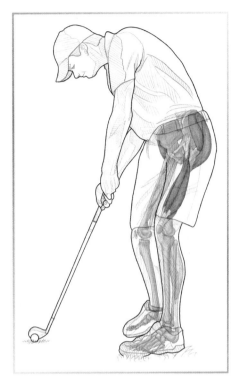

within the swing is sent to the ball at impact. This ultimately leads to a more powerful swing that results in increased distance.

---

## VARIATIONS

### Lateral Bounding With Medicine Ball

Using a medicine ball not only provides increased resistance but also creates a more intense balance challenge since the arms cannot be used for stability. Hold the medicine ball just in front of your chest with your elbows bent.

### Lateral Bounding With Turns

This simple addition will greatly challenge both your balance and stability as well as help you work on your golf turns. Once you land, place your arms across your chest and rotate your torso, first toward the stance leg and then to the opposite side.

# Overhead Throw on BOSU Ball

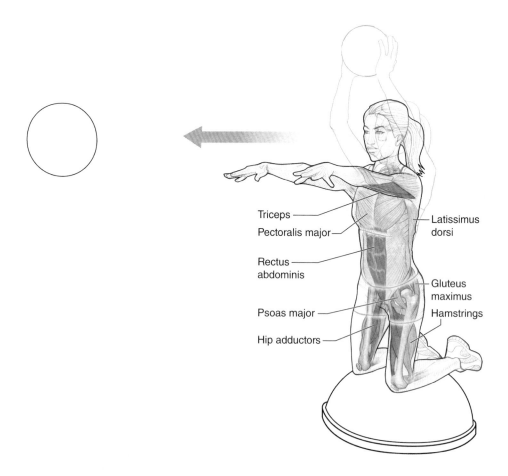

Triceps
Pectoralis major
Rectus abdominis
Psoas major
Hip adductors
Latissimus dorsi
Gluteus maximus
Hamstrings

## Execution

1. Kneel on the curved half of a BOSU ball. Toes are off the ground.
2. Hold a medicine ball over your head as for a soccer throw.
3. While maintaining your stability and balance, throw the medicine ball to a partner.
4. Catch the ball and repeat.

## Muscles Involved

**Primary:** Rectus abdominis, hip adductors, triceps

**Secondary:** Gluteus maximus, psoas major, hamstrings, pectoralis major, latissimus dorsi

## Golf Focus

Although the overhead toss is not a movement that mimics the golf swing, it is great for building strength and balance throughout the body simultaneously. One muscle group that athletes often ignore during their fitness training is the adductor muscles of the inner thigh. These muscles are very important for creating proper pelvis motion 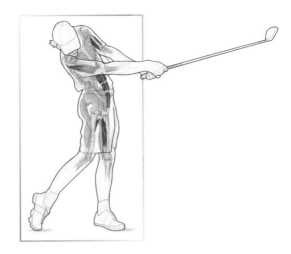 and core stability throughout the golf swing. By keeping your feet off the ground during this exercise, you really have to work the adductor muscles and all the muscles within the abdominal region. Another benefit of this exercise is that the body automatically assumes the golf setup posture at the hips and pelvis when kneeling on the ball. As such, this exercise is great for strengthening the muscles that help create stability of the pelvis and spine while maintaining your golf posture.

### VARIATION

### Overhead Mock Throw on BOSU Ball

When a partner is not available, you can get great benefits from performing this exercise without actually releasing the ball. Just kneel on top of the BOSU ball and make mock throws of the medicine ball by bringing it over your head into a soccer throw position and then, using both arms, bringing it out in front of your chest. Perform the movement at a speed that you are able to maintain proper balance on the BOSU ball. As you become better at the balance aspect of this exercise, increase the speed at which your arms move through the movement.

# Plyometric Push-Up

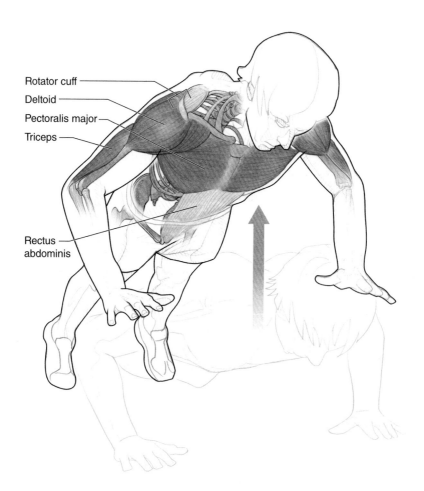

Rotator cuff
Deltoid
Pectoralis major
Triceps
Rectus abdominis

## Execution

1. Get into a normal push-up position with hands about shoulder-width apart.
2. Lower yourself down as for a normal push-up.
3. Push up as hard and as fast as you can so that your hands come off the ground.
4. Land with elbows slightly bent, and repeat.

## Muscles Involved

**Primary:** Pectoralis major, triceps, deltoid

**Secondary:** Rectus abdominis, rotator cuff

## Golf Focus

Most shots in golf do not require immense amounts of upper body strength and power. However, there are certain times when these fitness components become extremely important for your shot-making potential. One of the reasons that Tiger Woods is so good at scrambling is because he has the upper body strength and power to complete some very difficult shots. It is inevitable that some of your tee shots will end up in some really deep rough. Without enough strength, you will have no other option but to safely hit back out to the fairway, and even this can be challenging. Increasing the power in your upper body by doing plyometric push-ups will give you many more options after poor tee shots. You will be able to get back to the fairway much more easily, and you will also have more opportunities to go for the green from a terrible lie.

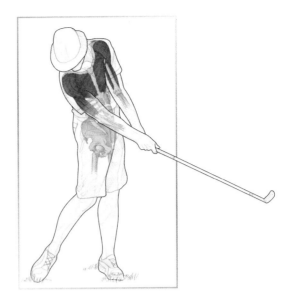

# VARIATION

## Supine Medicine Ball Throw on Stability Ball

This exercise will work the same major muscle groups, but it is much easier. Use a proper medicine ball weight so that the throw is challenging but the ball is easy enough to catch safely. Once you begin using larger medicine balls, progress to plyometric push-ups so that you don't get hurt throwing lots of weight. Lie on your back with your knees bent. Hold the medicine ball with both hands on top of your chest. Using both hands, throw the ball straight up into the air. Catch and repeat.

# Torso Throw on Stability Ball

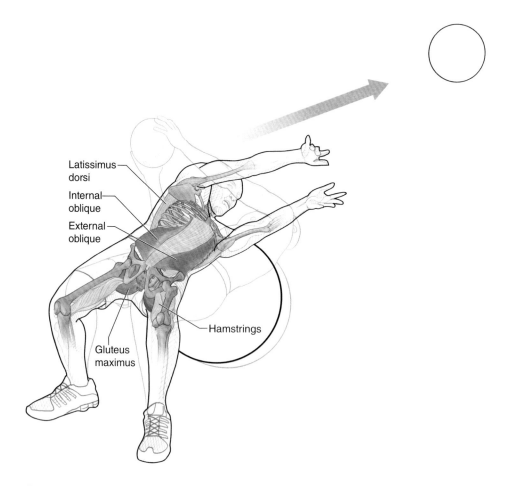

Latissimus dorsi

Internal oblique

External oblique

Gluteus maximus

Hamstrings

## Execution

1. Lie with your upper back on a stability ball and your arms above your chest.
2. Catch a ball thrown to you by a partner, and rotate 90 degrees away from the partner.
3. Rotate back toward the partner, and release the ball when your shoulders are stacked on top of each other and you are facing the partner.
4. Perform the desired number of repetitions and repeat, rotating to the other side.

## Muscles Involved

**Primary:** Internal oblique, external oblique, gluteus maximus

**Secondary:** Latissimus dorsi, hamstrings

## Golf Focus

To produce a repeatable, efficient, and powerful golf swing,
it is important to create separation between the pelvis and
shoulders while maintaining
stability within the hips, pelvis,
and core. In addition, once this
separation has been created, a
golfer needs to be able to close
the separation quickly as he
approaches impact. The torso
throw on stability ball exercise is
a great movement for any player
looking to develop the ability to
separate the upper and lower
body, develop stability during
movement of the torso, and gain
the ability to close the separation
created during the backswing
and onset of the downswing.

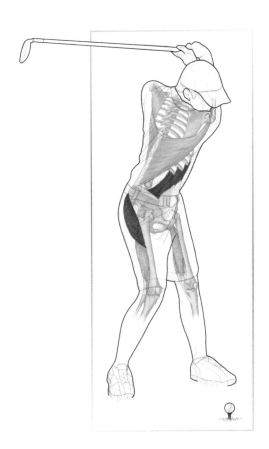

## VARIATION

### Torso Throw on Stability Ball With Tubing

A great variation of the torso throw exercise
is to perform this movement using a piece of
tubing when a partner is not available to
throw you the ball. Make sure the tubing
isn't too tight to begin with, and concentrate on making full turns on your shoulders
and maintaining a solid feel throughout
the core and shoulder regions.

# Opener Rotation

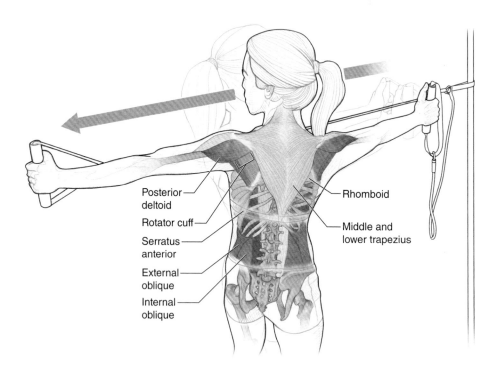

Posterior deltoid

Rotator cuff

Serratus anterior

External oblique

Internal oblique

Rhomboid

Middle and lower trapezius

## Execution

1. Attach tubing to a pole, and hold onto a handle in each hand. Arms are straight out in front of your chest, palms facing each other.
2. Rotate one arm, your head, and your torso as far as possible to one side.
3. Slowly return to the start position, and repeat with the other arm.

## Muscles Involved

**Primary:** Rotator cuff, posterior deltoid, internal oblique, external oblique

**Secondary:** Serratus anterior, middle trapezius, lower trapezius, rhomboid

## Golf Focus

During the downswing, power is generated by the legs and transmitted through the core and into the arms. When the energy generated within the legs reaches the shoulder complex, it is important that the muscles stabilizing the shoulder blade be strong and work in concert with the muscles of the core. The opener rotation is a great exercise to help strengthen the core and shoulder stabilizers simultaneously. Using a piece of tubing is a great way to improve your shoulder and core stability to help transfer the power from the ground through your torso and into the arms just before impact. In the illustration, you can see that the target-side shoulder blade is maintaining its descended position at the onset of the downswing. This position allows for proper stabilization and mobilization of the shoulder throughout the swing, allowing for maximal energy transfer to occur.

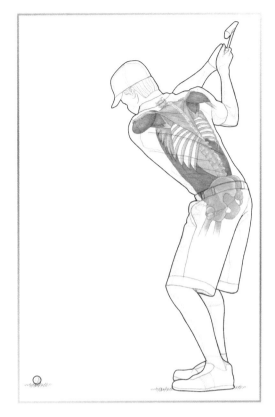

---

### Opener Rotation From a Golf Cart

The opener rotation is a great exercise to perform before playing a round of golf or practice round. We use this exercise quite often in the PGA Tour trailers. Although most amateur golfers don't have the luxury of working out in a gym before a round of golf, they usually have access to a golf cart. Try this exercise with the tubing attached to one of the poles on your cart for a great warm-up of your core and shoulders.

# Plyometric Front Squat

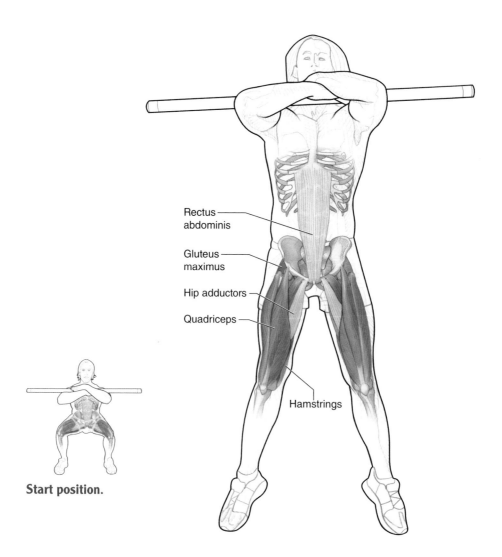

Rectus abdominis

Gluteus maximus

Hip adductors

Quadriceps

Hamstrings

**Start position.**

## Execution

1. Stand with legs about shoulder-width apart and feet slightly turned outward. Hold a bar across your chest with arms crossed to support the bar.
2. Knees should be above the ankles and not dropping in toward the center.
3. Jump up as high as possible while maintaining body control.
4. Land back in the starting squat position. As soon as your feet touch the ground, start the jump again.

## Muscles Involved

**Primary:** Gluteus maximus, hamstrings, quadriceps

**Secondary:** Rectus abdominis, hip adductors

## Golf Focus

As we have mentioned through-out this book, power needs to be generated by the legs driving into the ground. The plyometric front squat is a fantastic exercise to build powerful muscles throughout the legs and buttocks. We have all seen the best golfers in the world explode their pelvises just before impact. This pelvis drive helps anchor the golfer into the ground and allows for proper transmission of that power through the body into the club. Use this exercise to help produce more power in your golf game. Start with very little to no weight, and as you become stronger, add a little weight at a time. This is not an exercise where you will ever load up with a lot of weight. It is designed for light weight that can be moved quickly—just like the golf swing.

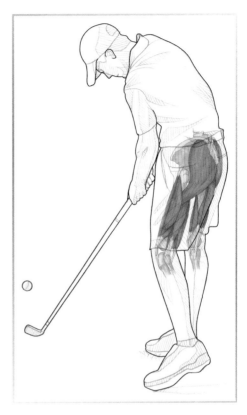

In the illustration, you can see the golfer creating a powerful extension through the pelvis and really taking advantage of the large muscles in the legs and buttocks to derive maximum energy from the ground up.

### VARIATION

### Front Squat

It is advisable to try the regular front squat before attempting the plyometric version of this exercise. When you can perform the front squat safely and with good movement, try the plyometric movement—first with no weight and then slowly adding a little weight as you feel comfortable.

# Plyometric Golf Throw to a Partner

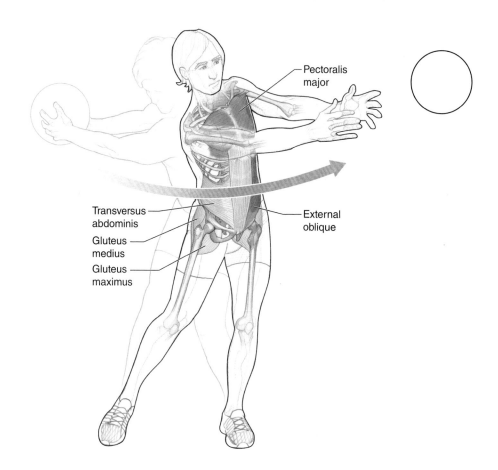

Pectoralis major

Transversus abdominis

Gluteus medius

Gluteus maximus

External oblique

## Execution

1. Stand in your golf posture. A partner stands directly to your left, holding a medicine ball. This is the start position.

2. Your partner throws the medicine ball to you. While tilting within your golf posture, catch the medicine ball as you rotate your torso and arms to your right.

3. In one smooth movement, decelerate the medicine ball, and then initiate movement back to your left by pushing your legs down to the ground to accelerate your arms and the ball back toward your partner.

4. Release the ball back to your partner and finish your rotation so you are in a full standing position.

5. Return to the start position and repeat for the desired number of repetitions.

6. Repeat, rotating to the other side.

## Muscles Involved

**Primary:** Internal oblique, external oblique, pectoralis major

**Secondary:** Gluteus maximus, gluteus medius, transversus abdominis

## Golf Focus

Once you come to the top of your back-swing, it is important to use your core to decelerate the movement away from the target and simultaneously use your legs to begin driving your pelvis toward the target. This is when true separation of the pelvis and shoulders occurs. Learning how to use the legs to initiate the downswing while concurrently creating separation of the pelvis from the upper body is an important aspect of developing power and efficiency during the swing. Golf throws help develop eccentric (lengthening) and concentric (shortening) power within the pelvis, core, and arms.

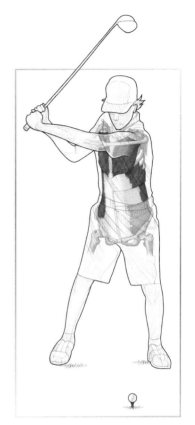

---

### VARIATION

## Golf Posture Throw to a Wall

When a partner isn't available, this exercise can be done by throwing the ball against a wall. Instead of catching the ball as you did in the main exercise, start the movement by holding the medicine ball in your golf address posture. Initiate the movement into your backswing as you would in your normal golf swing. Initiate the downswing through the legs, and release the ball toward the wall.

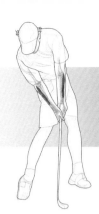

# PREVENTING INJURIES IN GOLF'S FIVE PROBLEM AREAS

**G**olf injury prevalence and physical location differ between amateur and professional golfers. Differences in swing mechanics, conditioning levels, number of swings taken (both during practice and on the course), and equipment use account for the differences seen among various players. Although numerous injuries can occur while playing golf, several are seen frequently. The most common sites of injury in golfers are the lower back, wrist, shoulder, elbow, and hip. The speed and force of the swing are often the cause of golf injuries, but they can also be attributed to a player's poor physical conditioning for the sport. Many touring professionals take hundreds of swings per day and are able to keep their bodies relatively injury free. However, many weekend golfers take only 100 swings in a day, and it completely wrecks their bodies. Why is this? Quite simply, the professionals have prepared their bodies for the sport both physically and technically so that they can avoid injuries and play in tournaments each and every week. Many of the exercises found throughout this book are the same exercises the professionals use to get their bodies in top shape for the golf swing. This chapter is dedicated solely to those areas of the body that suffer from the most injuries so that you can spend a little extra time and focus on them to keep yourself off the injured list.

Studies report that lower back injuries account for 63 percent of golf-related injuries in professional golfers and for 36 percent in amateur golfers. In general, rotation of the lumbar spine in the workplace has been directly correlated with lower back injury. Outside of the workplace, rotational movements have been indicated in up to 50 percent of lower back injuries. When these rotational movements are combined with forward bending of the spine, the likelihood of lower back injury is greatly increased. Knowing that the golf swing incorporates both of these movements, it is obvious why lower back pain is the number one injury for golfers. In everyday life, rotational movements are normally controlled, but the golf swing is not. In addition, the golf swing requires multiple joints to undergo near-maximal or maximal rotation for it to be performed efficiently. A loss of or excessive movement at any one of these areas will result in undesirable compensations within the kinetic chain. Is it any wonder the golf swing results in so many back injuries?

To put this all into perspective for you, the compressive forces found within the lower back are equivalent to eight times a person's body weight with each swing. That means if you weigh 200 pounds (90 kg), 1,600 pounds (720 kg) of compressive force go through your lower back every time you take a full swing! Running, which is considered a high-impact sport, normally produces compression of only three to four times a person's body weight. This comparison alone should make you start to consider how fit your body truly is to withstand these high forces in your spine with each swing.

Wrist injuries are also common. They often occur at the point of impact when the golf club comes into contact with something other than the ball. This could include the ground, a tree root, a buried rock, or the driving-range mat. Often, these types of injuries occur in amateurs when they hit a "fat shot." This is when the ground is struck before contact is made with the ball. In better golfers, wrist injuries are often secondary to playing in deep rough, where the longer grass grabs at the club head and hosel and rapidly decelerates the club head in a manner that is similar to hitting a fat shot. In either case, it is the rapid deceleration of the club, and therefore the wrist, that causes the injury. Since players can't always avoid hitting from situations that cause this rapid deceleration, they should prepare their wrists to deal with this intense force. Strengthening the wrists will not only help you prevent excessive loss of speed of the club head but also help keep your wrists from being strained to the point of injury. Once you have passed this point and injury has occurred, it is very difficult to play golf since each swing will send vibrations and force throughout damaged tissue in the wrist. This slows the healing process and can potentially make the injury worse. Therefore, the best plan is to prepare your wrists for any situation so that you have the strength to prevent these types of injuries.

The shoulder is another frequently injured body part among professional golfers, with injury to the lead shoulder occurring in up to 75 percent of cases. The shoulder is often referred to as the shoulder complex, and it is just that: complex! The anatomy and biomechanics involved in shoulder function are so intricate that many different deficiencies can lead to injury. Very large ranges of motion in a number of planes create an inherently unstable joint that relies predominantly on the soft tissues surrounding the joint for stability. If we consider the clavicle (collar bone), humerus (arm), and scapula (shoulder blade), these three bones alone are served by 20 muscles, with 95 sites of insertion. Many people concentrate on only a small number of these muscles when performing a fitness training session. As a result, the shoulder's mechanics are negatively affected. It is important to train the muscles you can't see in addition to the ones you can. Golfers usually experience pain in the shoulder because of an imbalance of shoulder musculature that prevents the joint from moving properly. This is why it is crucial to work every part of the shoulder complex equally in your fitness regime so that balance can be achieved. This will improve the range of motion of your shoulders as well as keep you from experiencing shoulder pain.

When people think of elbow injuries in golf, they automatically think of golfer's elbow. Sounds logical, right? Well, in fact, the most common elbow injury in golf is tennis elbow! In golfers, tennis elbow can occur on either the lead or trail elbow, although it is most common on the lead side. Gripping the club too tightly during the swing or altering the grip may result in changes to the amount of force generated by the forearm musculature. This excess force can overload the tissue and lead to elbow injury. Other common reasons for tennis elbow in golfers are the chicken-winging swing flaw on the follow-through and bending the elbow during the takeaway. Both of these will cause the golfer to eventually straighten the elbow with rapid force and overload the elbow tissues.

Golfer's elbow, on the other hand, refers to damage to the muscles and tendons in the area of the inside elbow. Most commonly, the trail-side elbow is affected. Early casting of the club in the downswing can produce a force that is too much for the muscles to handle. Repeatedly swinging with this poor technique can easily cause tissue damage and lead to pain with each and every swing.

The last area of injury that we are going to focus on is the hip. Although most golfers know that rotation of the hips, pelvis, and torso is necessary for an efficient swing, most do not have proper strength and movement in the hips. This lack of movement and strength not only causes you to produce a technically inefficient swing but also distributes awkward forces through the hips. The body is very smart and will find a way to move one way or another. The problem is that many times these compensation patterns are the reason for injuries. Asking the hips to move with speeds and motions they are not capable of will stress the muscles, ligaments, tendons, and joints in the area and begin causing pain. Pain in the hips makes it nearly impossible to produce proper rotation in the golf swing and to execute an efficient swing pattern.

Unless otherwise noted, perform 8 to 12 repetitions of the following exercises. For those that require free weights, resistance tubing, or cable machines, start with a low weight or resistance that enables you to complete 3 sets of 12 repetitions. Once you can easily complete 3 sets of 12 repetitions, increase the weight or resistance so you can complete 11 repetitions but struggle on the last one. Perform 2 or 3 sets of 8 repetitions for exercises that use only body weight. Once you can easily complete 3 sets of 8 repetitions, increase to 10 repetitions.

LOWER BACK

# Lunge Mobility Stretch

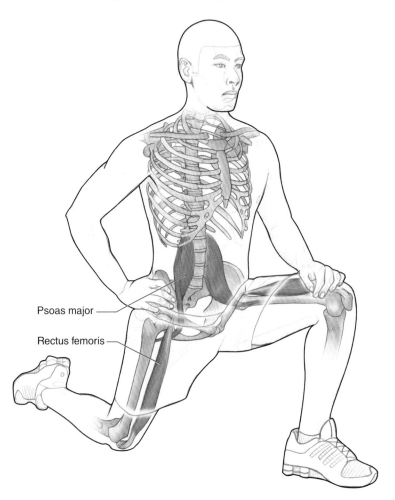

Psoas major

Rectus femoris

## Execution

1. Get into a lunge position with your left foot forward and your right knee back and on the ground.
2. Keep your back straight and chest out throughout the exercise.
3. Slowly move forward by bending your front leg.
4. When you feel a stretch in the upper and inner thigh of your back leg, hold for 5 counts.
5. Return to the start position, do the desired number of repetitions, and repeat with the opposite leg.

## Muscles Involved

**Primary:** Psoas major, rectus femoris

## Golf Focus

Lower back pain is an injury that runs rampant throughout the golf world. Because of the high level of force that translates into the spine with each swing, it is important to have all the relevant muscles working properly in order to protect the spine. This protection begins as soon as you address the golf ball. The proper angle of the spine at address sets you up for proper angles throughout the swing. Address the ball incorrectly, and your chances of having an efficient swing fall drastically. The lunge mobility stretch helps prepare two of the major muscles activated in the lower back and pelvis. If these two muscles cannot perform properly, you will not only lack the ability to address and hit the ball correctly but will also move closer to back injury with each swing.

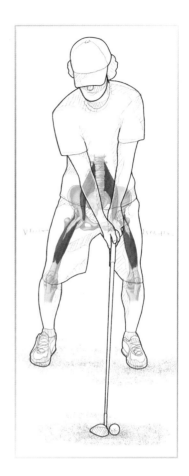

# Single-Limb Bird Dog

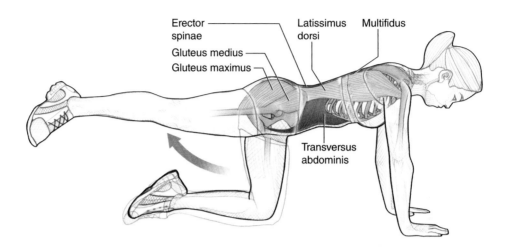

## Execution

1. Get on all fours with your hands under your shoulders and knees under your hips.
2. Keep your back and neck straight at all times.
3. Without moving your pelvis or back, lift your right arm and raise it straight out in front of you.
4. Return to the start position, and repeat with the opposite arm.
5. Next, lift your right leg and raise it straight out behind you.
6. Return to the start position, and repeat with the opposite leg.

## Muscles Involved

**Primary:** Transversus abdominis, multifidus, erector spinae

**Secondary:** Gluteus medius, gluteus maximus, latissimus dorsi, rhomboid

## Golf Focus

The bird dog exercise is one of the most utilized exercises for lower back pain rehab and strengthening, and for good reason. It not only helps strengthen many of the core muscles but also helps your body learn how to stabilize while moving your limbs. This becomes crucial in a sport such as golf, where stabilization of one body part must occur while other body parts are moving rapidly. Without the ability to produce these two in conjunction, injuries are much more likely. In the case of the lower back, it is very important to maintain proper spinal angles during the entire swing. Many golfers are infamous for their reverse-C finish position, which places undue stress on the lower spine. Strengthening your core musculature while allowing other body parts to move freely will help you maintain proper spinal angles throughout the swing and into your finish to help prevent lower back injuries.

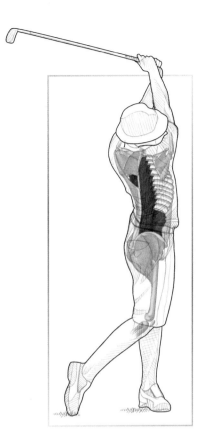

---

### VARIATION

## Opposite-Limb Bird Dog

This version of the bird dog is much more of a challenge. Maintain the same form and do the same movements, but move the opposite arm and leg at the same time. Keep the pelvis and lower back still to avoid tilting of the pelvis or arching of the spine.

# Knee-Down Front Plank

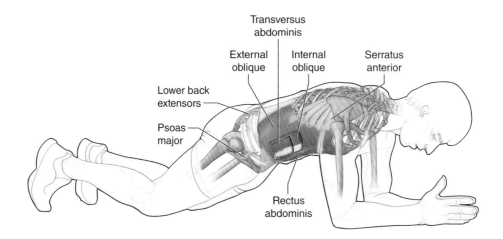

## Execution

1. Lie facedown with your arms bent and close by your sides.
2. Lift your body off the ground and tighten your abdominal and back muscles.
3. Your weight will rest on your forearms and knees. Continue looking down at the floor.
4. Hold the position for 15 to 20 seconds.
5. Make sure your lower back doesn't sag.
6. Don't forget to breathe while holding the position.

## Muscles Involved

**Primary:** Transversus abdominis, rectus abdominis, internal oblique, external oblique

**Secondary:** Lower back extensors, psoas major, serratus anterior

## Golf Focus

The most common body area to be injured or painful in golfers is the lower back. The abdominal plank position with the knees and forearms supporting the weight of the body is an easy low-impact exercise that is great for helping to keep the small muscles that protect the spine strong and functional. If you suffer from back pain or would like to prevent back pain from ruining your round of golf, this exercise is a must. The most important key to this exercise is to make sure your form is perfect. This ensures the correct muscles are trained and the lower back is protected.

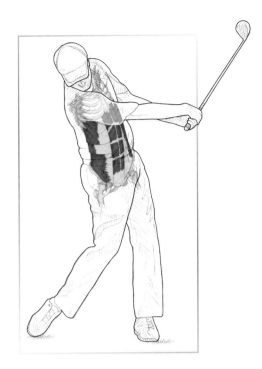

# Wrist Deviation

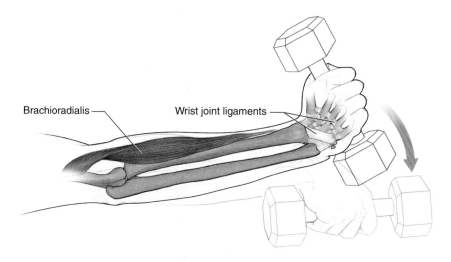

## Execution

1. While standing, hold a light dumbbell of 5 to 15 pounds in your right hand straight out in front of you.
2. Keep your right elbow straight and your right palm facing to the left during the entire exercise.
3. Slowly tilt your hand toward the floor.
4. Then slowly tilt your hand up as far as you can.
5. Repeat the desired number of repetitions, and then repeat with the other hand.

## Muscles and Ligaments Involved

**Primary:** Brachioradialis, wrist joint ligaments

## Golf Focus

Setting the hands properly is a very important part of the golf swing. Moving your hands and wrists incorrectly can cause you to compensate in many ways throughout the swing. As you bring the club into your back-swing, the wrists must hinge to set the club in the proper position before the downswing is initiated. If done incorrectly, then you will have to alter your swing plane to get the club face square again before impact. The downswing also requires a lot of wrist action as you rapidly release the club to prepare for impact. Golfers often injure their wrists because they cannot handle the stress of either a proper hinge or the release of the club. Wrist deviations not only strengthen the wrist to prevent these injuries but also help ensure that you have an adequate range of motion in your wrists.

### VARIATION

## Wrist Deviation With Golf Club

This exercise can also be done with a golf club, which can make it much more difficult. The more distance between your hand and the top of the club, the more difficult the exercise. This variation will strengthen the same muscles and will also help you get the feel of hinging with an actual club.

# Ball Breaker

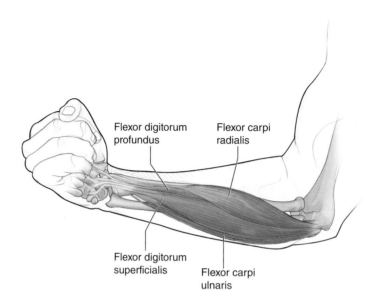

Flexor digitorum
profundus

Flexor carpi
radialis

Flexor digitorum
superficialis

Flexor carpi
ulnaris

## Execution

1. Stand with your right arm bent 90 degrees and a golf ball in your right hand.
2. Squeeze the golf ball as hard as you can.
3. Hold for 2 seconds and release.
4. Repeat the desired number of repetitions, and do the same with the left hand.

## Muscles Involved

**Primary:** Flexor carpi ulnaris, flexor carpi radialis, flexor digitorum superficialis, flexor digitorum profundus

## Golf Focus

Many people forget about strengthening their wrists, but the wrist is one of the most commonly injured body parts in golfers. The majority of the swings you take will not encounter a substantial amount of resistance upon impact. However, you will often need to power the club head through deep rough or even stop the club abruptly at impact. If your wrists are not strong enough to handle these forces, then injury will soon follow. Although many exercises indirectly provide some level of wrist strengthening, ball breakers directly increase the strength in your wrists. They will also help your wrists become accustomed to intense pressure for those shots when you have to cut through thick grass or stop a full swing suddenly.

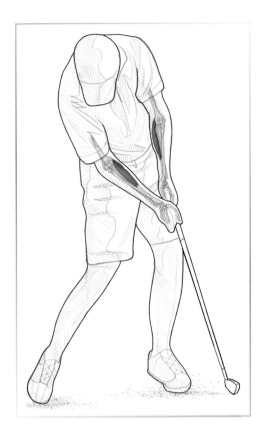

## SHOULDER
# Sidestepping With Shoulder External Rotation

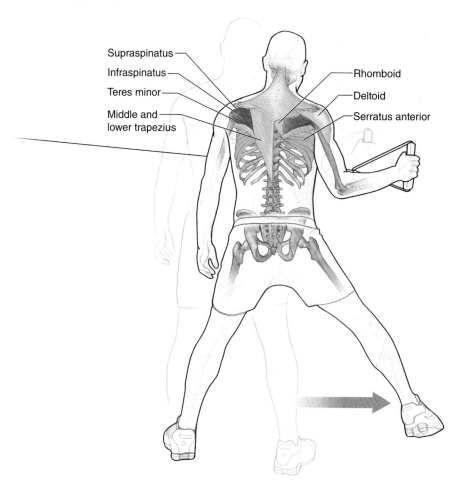

Supraspinatus
Infraspinatus
Teres minor
Middle and
lower trapezius

Rhomboid
Deltoid
Serratus anterior

## Execution

1. Stand with your legs shoulder-width apart and knees slightly bent.
2. Tubing should be hooked around a post or otherwise fastened.
3. Hold the tubing in your right hand with your right elbow bent to 90 degrees.
4. Rotate only through the shoulder to move your hand away from your body.
5. Maintain this arm position for the entire exercise. Your forearm, wrist, and hand should be held in a straight line at all times.
6. Sidestep to your right with both feet, and then return to your left.
7. Do the desired number of repetitions, and then switch to your other arm.

## Muscles Involved

**Primary:** Supraspinatus, infraspinatus, teres minor, subscapularis

**Secondary:** Deltoid, middle trapezius, lower trapezius, serratus anterior, rhomboid

## Golf Focus

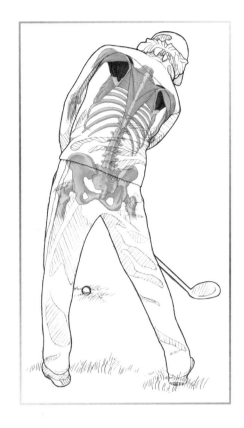

Whether they are caused by having weak muscles supporting the wrist, having poor technique, hitting a buried rock or other object when taking a deep divot, or hitting indoors on mats, wrist injuries are common in golfers of all skill levels. Technically, one of the problems golfers have is flipping or cupping the wrists through impact. When the wrist is flipped at impact, a hook is generated; when the wrist is cupped at impact, a slice is often the result. In both of these positions, significant losses in distance are seen because there is reduced compression of the golf ball. Sidestepping with shoulder external rotation helps build up strength in the forearm and wrist while also building up a great deal of strength in the shoulder stabilizers. This is a great exercise for people who have an injury or just want to get stronger through the wrists, forearms, and shoulders.

# Isolated Shoulder Retraction

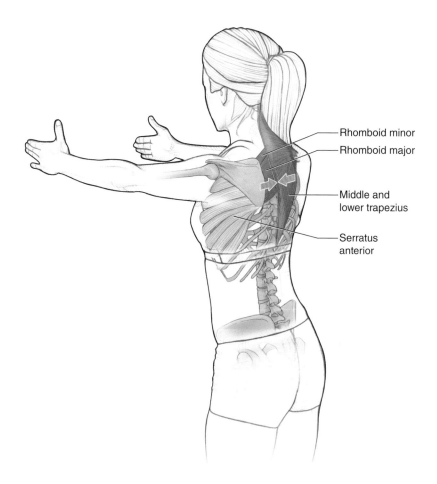

Rhomboid minor

Rhomboid major

Middle and
lower trapezius

Serratus
anterior

## Execution

1. Raise the arms to shoulder level in front of you.
2. Round your back as if trying to hug something in front of you.
3. Squeeze only the muscles between your shoulder blades to move the blades in toward each other; hold for 8 slow counts.
4. Don't shrug your shoulders up toward your ears. Keep them lowered throughout the exercise.
5. Repeat for the desired number of repetitions.

## Muscles Involved

**Primary:** Middle trapezius, lower trapezius, rhomboid major, rhomboid minor

**Secondary:** Serratus anterior

## Golf Focus

The shoulder is one of the most commonly injured areas in a golfer's body and is one of the areas contributing to poor technical form during the swing. When the shoulder blades are not able to move through a full range of motion, it places a tremendous amount of strain on the soft tissues (muscles, tendons, and ligaments) of the shoulder joint, upper back, and neck. Improper functioning of the shoulder blades will often show up in the golf swing, with the player unable to release the club through impact. Instead, the golfer will hold onto the club, and the target-side elbow will flare out in a chicken-wing appearance. This usually leads to a fade or slice ball flight. Learning how to move the shoulder blades through full protraction (blades move away from each other) and retraction (blades move toward the spine and each other) will help the golfer move the club more easily into the positions he wants and will decrease the stress placed on the upper back and neck.

# Push-Up Plus

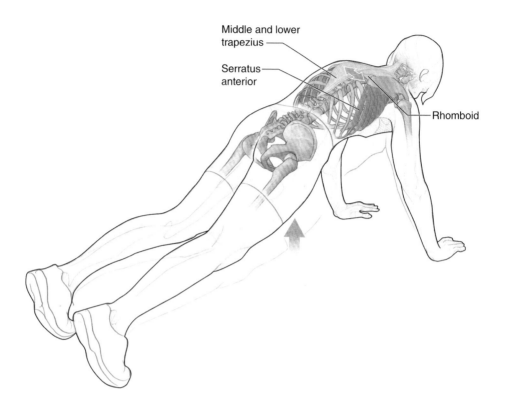

Middle and lower trapezius

Serratus anterior

Rhomboid

## Execution

1. Start in a push-up position.
2. Slowly push your shoulder blades as far apart as possible by lifting your upper back to the ceiling.
3. Slowly lower your back 1 inch (2.5 cm) by bringing the blades slightly together. Arms should remain straight. All movement should occur through the shoulder blades, not the spine.
4. Return to the start position and repeat.

## Muscles Involved

**Primary:** Serratus anterior

**Secondary:** Rhomboid, middle trapezius, lower trapezius

## Golf Focus

Many golfers have a problem making a full shoulder turn into the top of the backswing. Instead, they do a short turn and then lift the club with their arms to the top position. This lifting of the arms often occurs after the golfers have stopped turning, and it creates a steep plane. These golfers will have a difficult time creating an inside-out swing path and will often have deep divots.

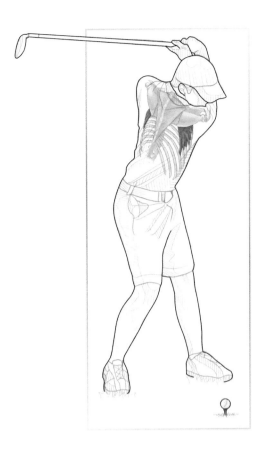

These players will also have difficulty releasing the club postimpact because their trail shoulder will not be able to wrap around their ribs. Instead, the shoulder blade gets stuck, and the players will remain in an exaggerated C-curve position throughout the deceleration process. This will place a great deal of stress on the lower back as well as the shoulders. The push-up plus exercise will help golfers learn how to separate and approximate their shoulder blades properly while developing core stability.

---

### V A R I A T I O N

## Full Push-Up Plus

When you are able to perform the push-up plus movement easily, you can attempt this exercise while lowering and raising yourself as you would in a regular push-up. This time, though, separate the shoulder blades near maximally when you are in the raised position with your elbows straight. You can also perform this exercise while resting on your knees.

# Sleeper Stretch

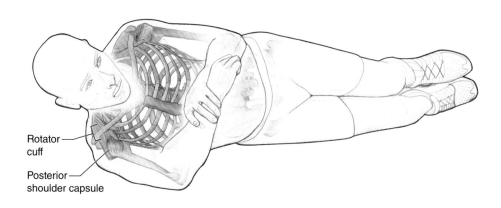

Rotator cuff

Posterior shoulder capsule

## Execution

1. Lie on your right side.
2. Bend your right elbow 90 degrees, and position the elbow at shoulder level.
3. Place your left hand on the back of your right forearm.
4. Push your left arm into the back of the right wrist to lower the right forearm toward the ground.
5. When you feel a deep stretch in the right shoulder, pause and hold for 20 seconds.
6. Repeat on the left.

## Muscles Involved

**Primary:** Posterior shoulder capsule

**Secondary:** Rotator cuff

## Golf Focus

Rotator cuff injuries are common in both professional and amateur golfers. One reason is that the capsule (the ligament-like structure that connects the shoulder blade to the arm bone) is excessively tight, specifically the back part of the capsule. When the capsule is tight, it pushes the arm too far forward in the shoulder joint, and the muscles that make up the rotator cuff are placed under more stress and are more likely to become injured. The sleeper stretch is a great way of maintaining some flexibility in this part of the shoulder, which helps prevent a loss of shoulder mobility and decrease the number of shoulder rotator cuff injuries. When performing this exercise, lean your torso slightly forward throughout the stretch so that the shoulder blade is not allowed to move. You want the movement to occur through the shoulder joint and not the blade.

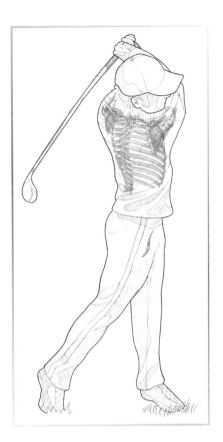

### VARIATION

### Sleeper Stretch Above and Below 90

Moving the elbow 10 to 15 degrees above or below the level of the shoulder when performing the sleeper stretch will help isolate different areas of the shoulder capsule and can be more efficient at creating more movement in the joint.

## ELBOW
# Dumbbell Forearm Extension

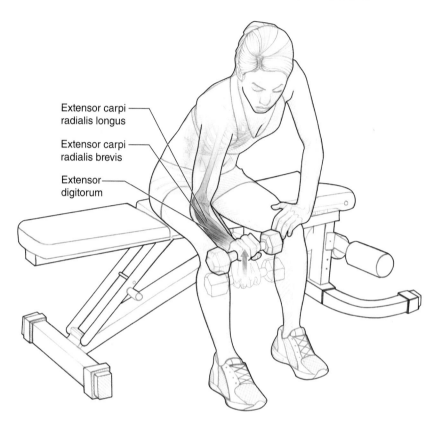

Extensor carpi radialis longus

Extensor carpi radialis brevis

Extensor digitorum

## Execution

1. Grab a dumbbell, sit on a bench, and place your right forearm on your right thigh so your palm is facing the ground.
2. Start with your wrist flat, and slowly lift your wrist into full extension.
3. Hold for 2 counts, and return to the start.
4. Repeat for the desired number of repetitions, and then perform the exercise on the left side.

## Muscles Involved

**Primary:** Extensor carpi radialis longus, extensor carpi radialis brevis, extensor digitorum

## Golf Focus

As you have probably learned by now, much of the power developed in the golf swing comes from the ability to create, maintain, and release proper body angles. Although the larger muscles of the body have a great potential for power creation, so too do the smaller muscles of the forearms. As the downswing begins, a golfer attempts to maintain or even decrease the angle between his arms and the club. The ability to maintain this angle during the downswing requires strength and control of the forearm muscles. However, many times the demands placed on these muscles exceed their abilities. This is a sure formula for injury. The dumbbell forearm extension is a great exercise to help train these muscles for strength so you can maintain club angles as well as prevent injury.

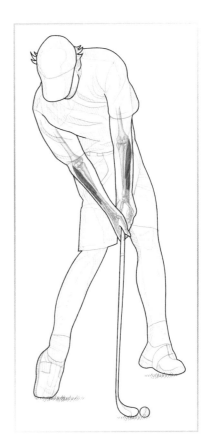

---

### VARIATION

### Barbell Forearm Extension

Exercise the same muscles simultaneously by using a barbell. This allows you to lift more weight and decreases some of the control that is necessary when using dumbbells. Make sure that all movement comes from the wrists and you are not allowing momentum to raise the weight.

# Dumbbell Forearm Flexion

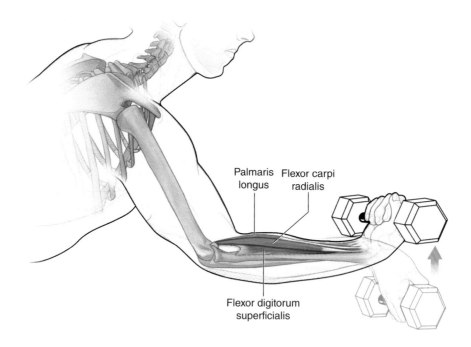

Palmaris longus

Flexor carpi radialis

Flexor digitorum superficialis

## Execution

1. Grab a dumbbell, sit on a bench, and place your right forearm in front of you so your palm is facing up.
2. Start with your wrist hanging down, and slowly lift your wrist into full flexion.
3. Hold for 2 counts, and return to the start position.
4. Repeat for the desired number of repetitions, and then perform the exercise on the left side.

## Muscles Involved

**Primary:** Flexor carpi radialis, flexor carpi ulnaris, palmaris longus, flexor digitorum superficialis, flexor digitorum profundus

## Golf Focus

Holding and maintaining various angles is important in many stages of the golf swing. However, if these angles are not released, then all that stored power will be wasted and cannot be transferred to the ball. During the beginning of the downswing, the goal is to create lag, or maintain the angle between the arms and the golf club. As the downswing progresses, you must release the club, increase its speed, and return the club head to its proper position to contact the ball squarely. The release of the club requires strength of the forearm muscles. The most common ways to injure these muscles are by overuse or by early release of the club. If you lose the angle between your arms and the club too quickly, the forearm muscles will undergo an excessive amount of force and will break down much quicker. The first way to avoid injury is to make sure you are not committing this swing fault, but you also must strengthen your forearm flexors to withstand the forces of club release. Even with proper swing technique, these muscles need to be able to withstand the thousands of shots you are going to take in your golfing career.

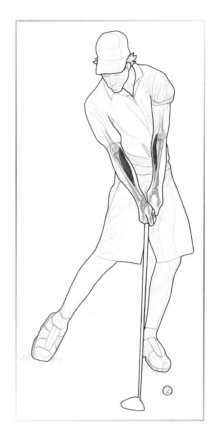

---

**VARIATION**

### Barbell Forearm Flexion

Exercise the same muscles simultaneously by using a barbell. This allows you to lift more weight and decreases some of the control that is necessary when using dumbbells. Make sure that all movement comes from the wrists and you are not allowing momentum to raise the weight.

# Dumbbell Rotation

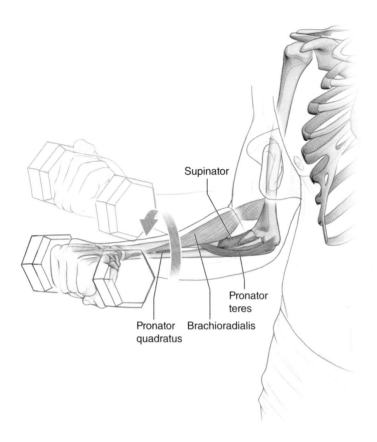

## Execution

1. Stand with a dumbbell in your hand and your elbow bent 90 degrees to your side.
2. Slowly turn your wrist and forearm fully so that your palm faces the ground.
3. Slowly turn the opposite way so that your palm faces up.
4. Repeat with the other arm.

## Muscles Involved

**Primary:** Pronator teres, supinator, pronator quadratus

**Secondary:** Brachioradialis

## Golf Focus

Many times when we think about the golf swing, we think about creating massive amounts of speed on the downswing. However, what happens after the club contacts the ball is also very important. Just after impact, the arms must stay extended and the hands must turn over. This wrist action requires strength in some of your forearm muscles. This rapid and precise control of the wrists needed after impact can cause injury to these forearm muscles. Dumbbell rotations will strengthen the muscles that help create proper club turnover. In turn, this strength will also help you prevent elbow injury caused by repeated swings and attempts to rapidly turn over your wrists.

---

### VARIATION

### Golf Club Rotation

This same exercise can be done with a golf club. Although the club is fairly light, this exercise is actually pretty difficult because of the length of the club. The longer the distance from your hand to the club head, the more difficult the exercise will be.

---

# Clam

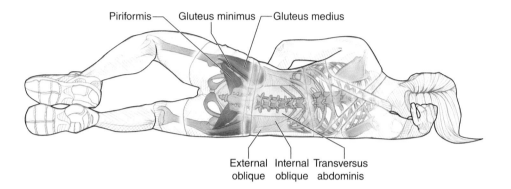

Piriformis — Gluteus minimus — Gluteus medius

External   Internal  Transversus
oblique   oblique  abdominis

## Execution

1. Lie on your right side with knees bent about 90 degrees; keep your ankles, hips, and shoulders all in line.
2. Keeping your feet touching, slowly lift your top knee up as far as you can.
3. Do not let your pelvis or lower back move at all during the exercise.
4. Return to the start position, repeat for the desired number of reps, and perform the exercise with the other leg.

## Muscles Involved

**Primary:** Gluteus medius, gluteus minimus, piriformis

**Secondary:** Internal oblique, external oblique, transversus abdominis

## Golf Focus

The hips play a huge role in the golf swing. Having pain or an injury at this joint can make it nearly impossible to move properly within the swing. Before strength or power can be considered for this area, you must first make sure you can correctly move the hips without moving the rest of your pelvis and torso. This is crucial for good hip mechanics and a good swing. As you move into your backswing, your lead hip needs to be able to open up independently of the rest of your body. This freedom of movement takes stress off the hip joint to help prevent injury and keep you rotating through the ball. Clams are a perfect exercise to make sure you are not only rotating the hip correctly but also maintaining a stable torso and pelvis.

# Figure 4 With Leg Extension

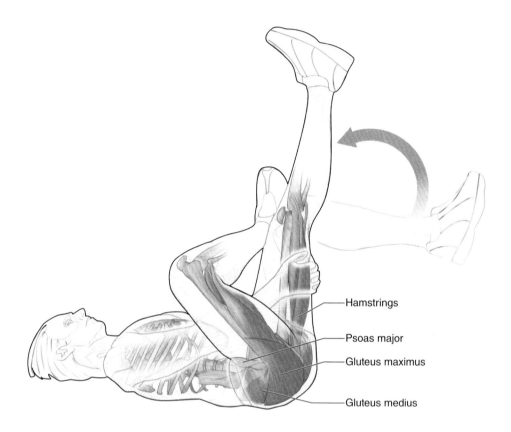

Hamstrings

Psoas major

Gluteus maximus

Gluteus medius

## Execution

1. Lie on your back and cross your right ankle over your left thigh, bending your left knee to approximately 90 degrees.
2. Hold your left thigh with both hands and bring your left thigh toward your chest until you feel a stretch in your left buttocks.
3. Gently increase the stretch in your buttocks by bringing your legs closer to your chest.
4. Straighten your left knee and feel the stretch in the hamstrings.
5. Hold for 20 to 30 seconds.
6. Repeat on the other side.

## Muscles Involved

**Primary:** Hamstrings, gluteus medius, gluteus maximus

**Secondary:** Psoas major

## Golf Focus

Many swing faults and lower back injuries occur as a direct result of poor flexibility within the chain of muscles, tendons, and ligaments that connect the bottom of the foot to your calf; from your calf to your hamstrings; and from your hamstrings into your pelvis and lower back. Many players have a problem covering the ball with the chest through the impact zone because of a flexibility issue within these tissues. The figure 4 with knee extension is a great exercise to stretch the hamstrings and the muscles on the opposite hip simultaneously. This exercise increases golf performance and decreases lower back and hip injuries.

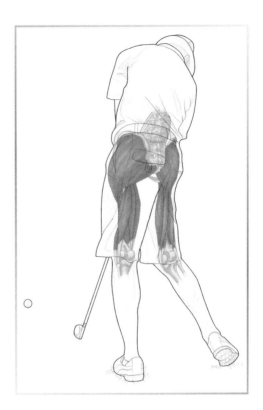

---

  **VARIATION**

### Figure 4 With Leg Extension and Foot Dorsiflexion

A more advanced version of this exercise can be performed by pulling the toes of the extended leg down toward your face. This stretches the tissue that connects all the way from your toes to your lower back. You may feel a burn on the outside of your left knee, a burn behind your knee, or just a more intense stretch in the calf muscles. It all depends on where your body has more restrictions in the ability of your tissue to stretch freely.

# EXERCISE FINDER

## Preventing Injuries in Golf's Five Problem Areas

# ABOUT THE AUTHORS

**D**r. Craig Davies is the director of nutrition and fitness for the Core Golf Academy at Orange County National in Orlando, Florida. He consults with the Canadian Junior National Golf Program, Netherlands National Golf Federation, Turkish National Golf Federation, and Trinidad and Tobago National Golf Association. He has worked with more than 50 professional golfers from the PGA, Nationwide, European, Canadian, LPGA, and Futures Tours.

Dr. Davies developed the golf exercise specialist and golf performance therapist certifications through Golf Performance Therapy, a company he cofounded, which is dedicated to providing complete physical analysis, cutting-edge performance therapy, fitness program design, and nutrition consulting for golfers. He was the keynote speaker at the inaugural Canadian National Golf Performance Summit in 2007 and is a Nike golf fitness mentor. Dr. Davies was born in Niagara Falls, Ontario, Canada, and now resides in Orlando, Florida.

**Dr. Vince DiSaia** is a strength and conditioning specialist and chiropractor specializing in fitness and therapy for elite golf performance. He received his level 2 certification as a medical golf fitness professional through the Titleist Performance Institute. Dr. DiSaia is cofounder of Triple Dynamix, Inc., a company that provides instructional DVD exercise programs for rehabilitating or strengthening the most commonly injured areas of the body. He has worked with amateur as well as touring professionals, including those on the Futures, LPGA, Asian, Japan, and PGA Tours.

Dr. DiSaia has also been KVest certified, which allows him to capture and analyze 3-D imaging of the golf swing. He helps players achieve complete golf fitness through performance therapy, biomechanical analysis, physical fitness, and nutritional optimization. He currently practices in Southern California, where he lives with his wife and two sons.

# ANATOMY SERIES

Each book in the *Anatomy Series* provides detailed, full-color anatomical illustrations of the muscles in action and step-by-step instructions that detail perfect technique and form for each pose, exercise, movement, stretch, and stroke.

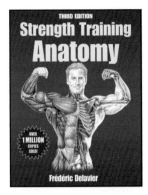

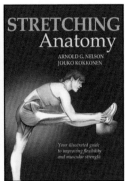

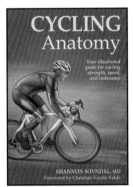

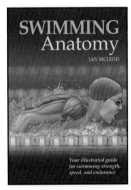

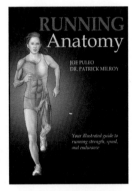

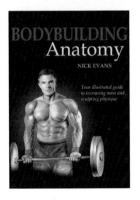

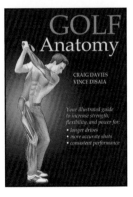

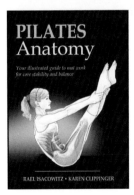

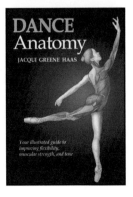

To place your order, U.S. customers call TOLL FREE **1-800-747-4457**
In Canada call 1-800-465-7301 • In Europe call +44 (0) 113 255 5665 • In Australia call 08 8372 0999
In New Zealand call 0800 222 062 • or visit **www.HumanKinetics.com/Anatomy**

**HUMAN KINETICS**
*The Premier Publisher for Sports & Fitness*
P.O. Box 5076, Champaign, IL 61825-5076